Along the
Garden Path

MORE QUILTERS AND THEIR GARDENS

JEAN & VALORI WELLS

PHOTOGRAPHY BY VALORI WELLS

C&T PUBLISHING

Developmental Editor: Barbara Konzak Kuhn
Technical Editor: Carolyn Aune
Copy Editor: Joan Cravens
Cover Designer: Christina Jarumay
Design Director/Book Designer: Christina Jarumay
Illustrator: Richard Sheppard © C&T Publishing, Inc.
Photography: Valori Wells; Steve Goldsmith (page 110, left column); Jane Marshall (page 100, top center)
Production Coordinator: Diane Pedersen
Production Assistant: Stacy Chamness

Library of Congress Cataloging-in-Publication Data
Wells, Jean.
   Along the garden path : more quilters and their gardens / Jean & Valori Wells.
   p. cm.
   ISBN 1-57120-118-1
   1. Quilting--Patterns. 2. Patchwork--Patterns.
   3. Appliqué--Patterns. 4. Gardens in art. I. Wells, Valori. II. Title.
   TT835 .W4617   2001
   746.46'041--dc21
                      00-011788

Published by C&T Publishing, Inc.
P.O. Box 1456
Lafayette, California 94549

Printed in China
10 9 8 7 6 5 4 3 2 1

Acknowledgments

Many people are involved in the writing of a book. We wish to thank those who helped us make *Along the Garden Path* a reality:

Eight quilters, who were an inspiration to us when we visited their gardens and who shared their quilting experiences with us.

Karin Hellaby, who introduced us to the English garden quilters included in the book and let us use her store, Quilter's Haven, as a home-base when we were in England.

John Pilcher of C&T Publishing, who introduced us to Rudolph DenHann and Wim Wagenmaster, BV, who put us in touch with Sarina Mayer de Feÿter in Axel, The Netherlands.

Barbara Ferguson, who was the "sewing fairy" helping us to finish projects and offering encouragement during deadlines.

Becky Goldsmith, who was teaching workshops at the store, then helped us again with her words and ideas on the afternoon she spent with us waiting for her flight.

The C&T Publishing family has been growing by leaps and bounds. We were fortunate to be able to work again with Barbara Kuhn as a developmental editor. She makes it so easy for us as authors to create the book as we see it intended. Thank you to Joan Cravens for copyediting our book. Christina Jarumay is the most creative book designer with whom we have ever worked. Her style and color sense lend an individuality that makes her books very unique. And thank you to Carolyn Aune and Joyce Lytle, who both know us and our way of interpreting quilt instructions. They make it all make sense mathematically. Richard Sheppard took our illustrations and made them clear and workable. Thank you to Todd and Tony Hensley for believing in us and providing a place for quilters everywhere to share their talents.

Our Stitchin' Post staff of twenty-three is invaluable as our sounding board when auditioning ideas, as well as putting up with us when we are on a tight schedule. We couldn't do it without them.

And last, but not least, thank you to John for his ongoing support of our varied pursuits (especially during deadlines).

Dedication

To Mother Earth for Her bountiful goodness, which we all enjoy. She is an inspiration to us whether we are observers or participants in rearranging what She provides us.

TABLE OF

C O N T E N T S

Preface

Is there anything more relaxing than napping under a handmade quilt or enjoying a garden in the sun? To us they are kindred pleasures. Planning and planting a garden takes patience and time, as does conceptualizing and creating a quilt. With both, we keep color, texture, and shape in mind. With both, we reap what we sow, or sew—lasting beauty and serenity.

Jean and Valori have been friends of mine for years. Jean loves gardening, while Valori relishes photography, and both care passionately about quilting. Watching Valori leaning off ladders, lying on her stomach or bending over a blossom to give us a bee's-eye view is a joy. Jean, all the while, is gathering props and searching for unseen treasures in the garden to capture with the camera, to show us the rewards of cultivating a garden and the connections between gardening and quilting.

A garden, be it large or small, is in our souls. In reading a good book or just plain relaxing in a garden, we are able to look at life in a different manner; the problems that seemed so important come into focus and we are able to come away refreshed. A stroll along a garden path with all of its color and splendor, or a walk in the woods with its majesty, adds to our well being.

In *Along the Garden Path*, Jean and Valori give us a stimulating look at gardens we would otherwise not see, and show us how gardening inspires the creativity in quilters. In it, we see how this wonderful pastime nourishes the souls of us all. Elbert Hubbard wrote *If I had but two loaves of bread, I would sell one of them to buy white hyacinths to feed my soul.* Now you can feed your soul with *Along the Garden Path*.

Margaret Peters
Artist, Teacher, Author

Introduction

Gardens and Quilts—Journeys of Discovery

 ourneys of creativity and discovery—quilting and gardening are parallel adventures, pleasing to the senses, challenging to the mind, and rewarding to the spirit.

Paths in the garden are much like the paths we take in quilting. They invite and direct us into a special world. In the garden, who knows what is down a hillside path, around a corner, under a tree? What will we discover on our journey? As a quilter, the odyssey begins with discoveries and decisions about design and color. The path may lead us to a new technique for piecing or appliqué, an experiment with colors, or an exploration of new borders. Our instincts and experiences lead us on our quest.

Mother Nature provides us with inspiration and ideas to last a lifetime. As quilters and gardeners we draw from Her colors and shapes, capturing in our quilts the color combinations generated in our gardens. The lupine growing around Jean's pond, for example, inspired Valori's quilt *Tango in the Garden*. Valori used the natural palette and, working from photographs, studied the proportions of the colors to determine how to place them in her quilt. The real flowers suggested a style of fabric that would glow in the quilt as the garden blossoms do against the natural green.

Quilting gardeners often explore different styles, too. Linda Sackin's urban California garden, for example, has a cottage look, with colorful small details that delight the eye. The coral tree in this garden, with its joyous abundance of flowers around the trunk, translates beautifully into her watercolor quilt. Linda's British Columbia island home, on the other hand, features a garden that is rustic and natural in style, and so are the quilts it inspires.

Discoveries in the garden may direct many a quilt design. When we are in the garden, we feel that we are unearthing things for the very first time. The joy of discovery may lead one to an idea for a quilt.

Become an observer of nature and the relationships that you see. A color combination, the way light reflects at dusk, the shape of a leaf—all may be adaptable for quilting. Trust your memories to lead you through the design process when you are quilting. Rely on what you see and like. Observations and recollections are dependable guides, proven paths to follow in your quilt odyssey. The magic of the garden will spill over into your quilts.

The quilters in *Along the Garden Path* have all been influenced by their gardens. Some were quilters first, others gardeners first. Wherever their journeys began, they feel a connection between the two pastimes. They believe that when you make a quilt you plant a vision, one that sprouts in the mind's eye and grows in fabric.

General Instructions

Designing a Quilt

Start with an idea, such as a snapshot, a picture from a magazine, or an image you have sketched. Collect ideas and study them, learning all you can about the relationship between the colors, shapes, and textures. Explore your subject matter with enthusiasm. Be open to all the possibilities. Embrace the challenges. They will lead you to new and better ideas.

Think about the potential size of your quilt. Will it be horizontal or vertical? What does the subject matter tell you? Is there a space in your home in need of a quilt? Sherry Morris' stairwell, for example, called for a long, narrow quilt. She used the stairwell to set her design parameters. Her collection of antique redwork quilts inspired her choice of the flowers of the month embroidered in red thread. They fit perfectly into the Drunkard's Path blocks, set on point to represent her iron-work fence.

Do you envision a landscape or a meadow, a single flower or a bouquet from a summer garden? Ask yourself whether the idea calls for a specific style of piecing. Becky Goldsmith wanted to capture the magic of individual flowers, so she chose to use appliqué, her signature technique. Solid colors sharpen the flower shapes. Had she wanted a more impressionistic look, she might have pieced the bouquet using printed cottons.

Often, a familiar piecing technique or style enables you to be comfortable enough that you can concentrate on exploring color possibilities. Lin Patterson's small Log Cabin block, for example, provided just this opportunity. At ease with the techniques used to create the blocks, she focused on color. Her hand-dyed fabrics represent the colors in the garden. Lin stitched them into what, at first glance, appears to be simply a contemporary Log Cabin wall hanging. The title, however—*Buttercups in My Garden*—calls attention to the golden blossoms in her garden beds, translated into small yellow squares in the centers of the blocks.

Style also suggests tone or mood, anything from whimsy to formality. *Lettuce in the Garden* by Jean is a play on words for her pieced and buttonhole-stitched quilt. It reflects her whimsical awareness of all the creatures—especially rabbits and deer—who want to get over or under the fence into her vegetable garden. From this idea the quilt was born. (It could have been entitled "Let Us in the Garden.") Buttonhole-stitch appliqué has a casual feeling that works well with this playful idea.

For her *Cottage Basket* quilt, Jinny Beyer selected a traditional Basket block. It showcases her floral-designed fabric and is in keeping with her quilting. The colors are misty, as were the colors in her garden on the rainy day that we photographed the quilt.

Exploring a variety of options when designing a quilt, whether you intend to create a traditional, appliqué, or contemporary design, is important. All of the techniques, alone or in different combinations, are possibilities in quilt design. Avoid limiting yourself.

From Inspiration to Paper

We find it useful to draft the desired size of the quilt onto graph paper. You will see the relationships in and between the spaces and can decide whether the design matches your vision. If it does not, explore making changes. Make the quilt vertical, for example, instead of horizontal as originally planned.

We let the composition direct this part of the quilt. In Valori's quilt, lupine would have a different feel portrayed horizontally because they are tall, stately flowers. To capture the essence of the whole flower, you would make your quilt more vertical. Val's color arrangement creates a vertical feeling.

Next, tape tracing paper over the graph and color the design using colored pencils. Try several color possibilities. There is value in spending time in this part of the process; it is "possibility thinking." Take another look at your photos or sketches. Have you omitted anything that you wanted to include?

Auditioning Fabrics

Selecting fabrics is the most enjoyable part of the process for many quilters. Is collecting fabrics your passion? Now is the time to dig into your treasures, looking for any fabric that could possibly work in your design. Keep your options open, remembering that you can reject something later in the quilting process.

Organize fabrics into color groups. If you have followed the guidelines above, you will find that you have several styles of fabric, from batik to hand-dyed to traditional calico. The next step is to think about the mood you want your quilt to convey. Fabric style is an essential element in establishing mood.

Make sure you have a full range of values if that is appropriate for your quilt. (Many of today's fabrics are of medium value.) In *Lettuce in the Garden* Jean knew that the pieced background behind the vegetables

needed to be lighter and duller than the appliqué colors in order to highlight the appliqué. To achieve the desired effect, she selected fabrics in a variety of values. Don't be afraid to step up the intensity of color. High-intensity fabrics, mixed with the other colors, can sometimes add just the spark your quilt needs. Brighter or lighter shades can act as accents.

Envision your fabrics cut up into small pieces as they will be in the quilt. Then decide what you need to make your color palette complete. Keep the rejected fabrics handy—they may work in the quilt later on.

Refer often to your photographs or sketches (design ideas) to analyze the relationships between colors. We call these "reference photos" and pin them on the design wall when working.

Design Elements

As in a beautiful garden, design elements in a beautiful quilt work together.

Balance is important in color placement and structure. You can see this easily if you have used yellow in only one place on the quilt or if all of the small piecing is in one area rather than spread around. Your design will look and feel unbalanced or lopsided. Trust yourself. Look at the quilt with a fresh eye. What looks fine on paper may need adjusting in fabric.

Color and texture go hand in hand because we are using fabric. Textural prints that represent lines and shapes in nature are effective in garden quilts.

Repetition is natural in quilting because many designs are repeated blocks. Look at your photograph or sketch for elements that can be repeated in the quilting as well. Is there a leaf shape or flower petal you can use as a quilting motif? Colors will automatically repeat themselves, but be conscious of this design element. Repetition of a variety of elements will give the quilt unity.

Stitching the Quilt

Guidelines for quilting are included for each quilt. As you read the instructions for each project, you will find additional instructions related to that specific quilt.

Cut pieces and stitch them accurately, using ¼-inch seam allowances, to ensure that points and corners of pieces meet correctly. Press seam allowances toward the darker fabric whenever possible.

We like to press any major seam, which means we are pressing often. We avoid using steam in the iron until seams are all together for a unit. Spray starch adds a crisp finish once the entire quilt top is assembled. It also makes machine-quilting easier.

Let the quilt take on a life of its own. Think of yourself as the facilitator: you are doing the hard work of cutting and sewing. Look often at what you have done, and consider how it is going. Is it turning out as you imagined? Do you need to make adjustments? Before making major changes, sleep on your ideas. Look at the quilt the next day to see whether an adjustment is still necessary. Allow yourself to be proud of what you are in the process of creating.

Finishing

When selecting a filler for your quilt, keep several things in mind. First, choose a batting that is appropriate for the end-use of the quilt. For example, if you are making a wall hanging, you want it to lie flat against the wall after it is quilted, so choose a flat batting. The filler also should be compatible with the fibers in the fabrics. Think, too, about the style of quilting you plan to do. Will your design be hand-quilted or machine-quilted? Which batting is suitable for this? How far apart can the lines of quilting be on the batting you have selected? Is the distance in keeping with the design you have in mind and the quilt's end-use?

Assembling the quilt layers correctly is important too. Try to find a table that you can work on, so you can clamp the backing to the table or tape down the edges so the fabric is taut but not tight. Layer the batting on the backing, patting out any bubbles.

Finally, add the top, making sure the edges are straight rather than distorted. (It is easier to quilt out extra fullness in the center of the quilt than it is to fix edges that ripple.) Thread or pin-baste the three layers together 3 inches to 4 inches apart.

Quilt Designs and Quilting

At the beginning of the design process, when you are looking at the photographs, start thinking about how to incorporate quilting lines into the overall design. The stitching that holds all the layers together is as important a part of the quilt as the color and piecing choices.

Study your subject matter for simple shapes that can be repeated. Trace the shapes using tracing paper, then enlarge or reduce them as necessary using a copy machine. Find ways to simplify the shapes or your idea, so you can quilt continuously. In *Tango in the Garden* actual leaves from the plant were copied and adapted. The flower design was then simplified and used for the quilting.

Quilting by hand or machine is a personal choice. If you choose to machine-quilt, a walking- or even-feed foot is good for straight lines and gentle curves. For more complex designs, lower the sewing machine's feed dogs and use an embroidery foot. It allows greater flexibility than a traditional foot, so you can move the fabric from side to side as well as backward and forward. Use interesting threads to carry out your ideas, as do many of the quilters in this book.

Binding

Binding is an individual matter. Each of the quilts in the book was bound a little differently than the others, but all look equally great. For each of the quilts we allow a 2½-inch-wide binding strip, which is ample for any method. When appropriate, we include specific binding instructions.

Enjoy your journey through the gardens in *Along the Garden Path*, experiencing their makers as both quilters and gardeners!

Huntington Beach, CA, United States
and Cortes Island, B.C., Canada

Two Garden Lives

Linda Sackin leads a double life as a gardener. Her home in Huntington Beach, California is in a neighborhood and the garden is suburban, watered by irrigation. Her Cortes Island garden in Canada is wild and natural, nourished by rainfall. Despite their differences, however, both display Linda's style, especially her love of flowers and winding pathways that draw the visitor into and through the plantings.

Outside Linda and her husband Paul's California home, a large coral tree almost as tall as the two-story house bids you welcome. The brick planter at its base is filled with ranunculus, Shirley poppies, yellow iris, and larkspur. The reds, yellows, oranges, and touch of blue in the flowers are a palette for a quilter. Beyond the tree, a wrought-iron gate opens to an atrium filled with ferns and orange lilies. From the tropical mood of the atrium, you walk through another opening into a flower-filled country garden. Linda's creative talents are everywhere, giving the garden its unique spirit and style.

Linda does not limit herself to accent flowers in clay pots. She fills old wheelbarrows, wicker baby carriages, metal pots, tea kettles, and baskets that draw you through her garden, from one delightful scene to another. These intimate plantings showcase the flowers, creating color combinations that could be subject matter for a quilt. The style of each container becomes part of the magic seen in this setting.

Blossom-filled containers reminded us of the floral fabrics that line Linda's sewing room shelves and her guest bathroom shelves. As quilters, we are seeing the beginnings of a design as we stroll through her garden.

Trickling water lures you along the brick-lined paths to a large birdbath fountain with two frogs. It sits serenely amid a bed of poppies, stocks, and anemones, creating a sanctuary away from the city. Throughout the flowerbeds are bits and pieces of Linda's collectibles: watering cans, hand-painted signs, sculptures. Comfortable wicker chairs with vintage fabric pillows provide a relaxed setting, a place to enjoy the garden and look beyond to boats on the water.

After quilting and gardening, making birdhouses is Linda's favorite pastime. Look for them everywhere in her gardens: atop a shelf or fence, perched in a tree, or tucked into a flowerbed.

She makes her birdhouses of old or new wood, creating cottage-style homes for her California garden and rustic houses for the island. Despite her efforts, birds have yet to move in. It will be a great day when they do!

In her California garden, Linda amends the soil yearly just as she does in Canada. Lacking a plot for vegetables, she works them into the flowerbeds, creating a crazy-patch quilt of greens and flowers. The lettuce and other green textures are restful next to vivid florals such as anemones and nasturtiums.

Flower colors take on new meaning in the garden. Red may be passionate, pink romantic and old-fashioned. Yellow can be soft and buttery or bright and intense, especially next to the yellow-green eyes of the gloriosa daisies. Magenta and orange are hot, drawing the eye, while blues sit quietly, elegantly in the background.

Both gardens feature brilliant orange nasturtiums, edible flowers that thrive even when unattended, and stems and foliage as interesting in color and shape as the flowers.

In the late spring Linda and Paul head north to their Cortes Island retreat in British Columbia. The only way to reach the island is by boat or sea plane. A generator provides electricity for the cabin. With the forest as a backdrop Linda enhances Mother Nature's plan by planting wildflowers amid the ferns and ground cover.

Cortes Island gardening is a challenge. "I sometimes think the rocks have babies overnight," says Linda of the stony soil. Bringing in mulch is not an option, so she amends the soil using buckets of seaweed. Perennials that re-seed themselves thrive better than other plants.

From the wooden deck around the house, you can see the fir trees rising from the ferns and bushes on the ground. Red strawflowers enhance the setting. Wild roses grow naturally in this rainy environment. Linda's birdhouses are everywhere. Each is a little different from the other. She combines rustic wood scraps, branches, and twigs to make these interesting structures.

White daisies with long, beautiful petals and yellow centers are natural to the area, growing wild among the rocks and trees. The daisies reseed themselves, reappearing each spring after the cold winter. In bloom for most of the summer, they are as interesting from the underside as they are from the top.

When Linda began her garden on the island, the deer were a problem, gobbling up new plants for breakfast, lunch, and dinner. She put up netting and, as she waited for more permanent fencing, she planned paths everywhere on the property, creating the structure for what was to come. Taking her cue from the natural environment, Linda selected accent fences made of twigs and sticks rather than pickets as in California. Paths were rock-lined using stones from the property. Linda's two gardens have grown and matured through the years, giving her year-round inspiration.

Tip

Mulch your flower beds. It keeps the ground moist and cuts down on weeds. Most soils need yearly doses of mulch.

Come Sit by the Coral Tree...
And Smell the Flowers!

LINDA SACKIN
35" x 39"

A large coral tree surrounded by a brick planter overflowing with flowers welcomes you to the Sackin's home. Linda chose this scene as the project she would create in Jean's garden-quilt design class. Wanting to create an impressionistic style, she chose to use a grid of squares on point.

Some of the squares were split into half-square triangles and used horizontally and vertically in the quilt to create details.

This technique allows you to focus on specific flowers as well as to create the impression of the tree.

To add detailing to the tree, Linda couched yarn on the tree trunk and made dimensional leaves from organza. She used a brick fabric for the first border to depict the planter at her home. The final border is a simple green print that serves to frame the wall quilt.

COME SIT BY THE CORAL TREE...AND SMELL THE FLOWERS!

Materials

You need a variety of fabrics for this impressionistic quilt to represent the different elements in the picture. The tree uses greens, browns, *and* some "transition fabrics" with green and brown in them. Transition fabrics bridge areas in a quilt, such as the leaves and branches in a tree or the leaves and petals in a flower. They create an illusion, so the eye sees the lines in the print rather than the seam lines. Select large- and small-scale floral fabrics to represent the flowers. You also need floral fabrics for the flower garden.

- 2 yards total of a wide variety of fabrics for the tree and garden
- $1/4$ yard for first border
- $3/4$ yard for second border and binding
- $1/8$ yard each of two shades of green organza for tree embellishment
- Small amount of thin brown yarn for tree embellishment
- $1/2$ yard paper-backed fusible web
- $1 1/3$ yards for backing
- 39" x 43" batting

Cutting

Cut ten to twelve 2" squares from each of the prints. More will be cut as needed. To speed cutting, layer up to five fabrics, cut a strip 2" wide, then cut it into 2" squares. For half-square triangles, cut a $2 3/8$"-wide strip into squares and cut them diagonally.

To individually cut a particular flower or leaf, trace the square and half-square patterns on page 31 onto template plastic and cut out. Position the plastic over the flower or leaf and cut around it.

First border: cut two strips $1 1/2$" x $26 1/2$" for the top and bottom, and two strips $1 1/2$" x $32 1/2$" for the sides.

Second border: cut two strips $3 3/4$" x $28 1/2$" for the top and bottom, and two strips $3 3/4$" x 39" for the sides.

Instructions

1. Begin by placing 14 squares on point across the top of a flannel design board, to represent the foliage in the tree. Next, place 15 squares down one side. Refer to the photograph to see where the tree ends and the flowers begin, and place fabrics accordingly. Once the top and side of the quilt are set, begin filling the remaining space as if you were putting a puzzle together.

2. Cut more squares and triangles as needed, keeping in mind that half-square triangles can be placed horizontally or vertically to create more detail.

3. Once you are happy with the design, stitch together the individual half-square triangles into squares. Press and trim the points.

4. Stitch squares together into diagonal rows, then join the rows. If you stitch from the top down on the first row, stitch from the bottom up on the next row to prevent the quilt from stretching in one direction. Press the seams in one direction.

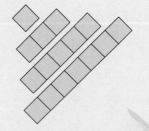

5. Use a ruler and trace a line around the quilt edges to make a 26" x 30" rectangle. Stay-stitch (single line of stitching) on this line to stabilize the bias edge. Measure $\frac{1}{4}$" from the line and trim off excess fabric. The rectangle should measure 26 $\frac{1}{2}$" x 30 $\frac{1}{2}$".

6. Add the first border to the top and bottom, then to the sides. Add the second border in the same manner.

7. Place yarn over the tree trunk, and tack it in place using matching thread.

8. For leaves, fuse together two shades of green organza. Cut leaf shapes, then lightly singe the edges using a candle, and tack leaves to the tree. Linda embellished the tree using 40 leaves.

9. Linda stitched-in-the-ditch diagonally in both directions to quilt the quilt.

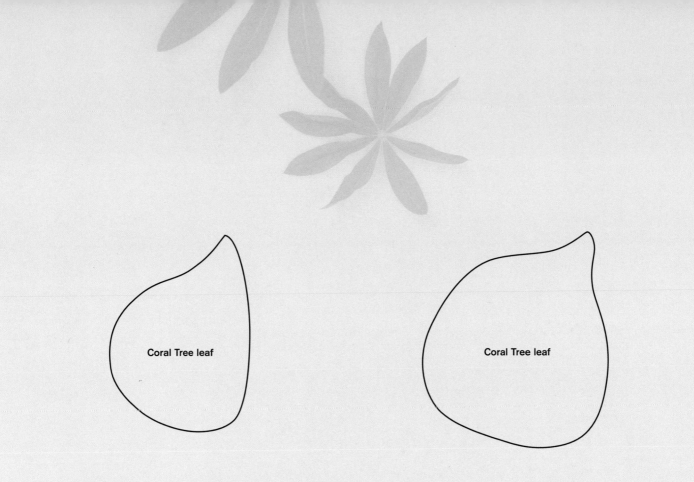

Coral Tree leaf

Coral Tree leaf

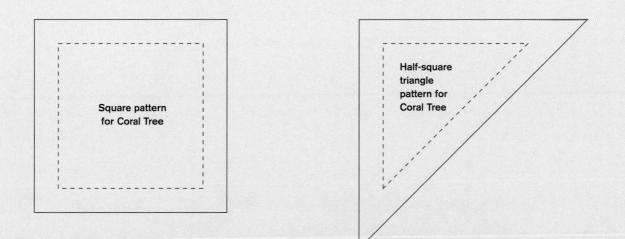

Square pattern
for Coral Tree

Half-square
triangle
pattern for
Coral Tree

LIN PATTERSON

Eye, England

English Country Garden

D riving through the English countryside, along a narrow road bordered by Queen Anne's lace as tall as the car, we turned into the approach to Lin Patterson's 600-year-old timber-gabled home and found ourselves in a field of yellow buttercups and lavender orchids. Big trees surround this flower-filled meadow, and beyond are bridges and ponds and fields of grass—so many places for children to play and dream. We felt we had stepped back in time.

Seven years ago, when the Pattersons moved in, the house had no garden. It stood amid grass, wildflowers, trees, and rubble. Lin and her husband planted a small patch by the back door first. Now the garden explodes around the house, reaching to the barn—a landscape of lively blues, reds, oranges, and yellows.

Intensity and contrast are important in both Lin's garden and her quilting. The colors in her quilts reflect her surroundings. The bright flowers in front of the house are a study in texture as well as color. Variety and intensity here create a dynamic, unpredictable garden.

For Lin's fortieth birthday, friends brought rose bushes for her garden. Planted in snowy November, the bushes were laden with blooms by early summer. As she tends her roses, Lin knows each represents the heart of a friend.

In this relaxed English garden, the Pattersons have taken their cue from the natural environment. Plantings fit the contours of the land. Lin works mostly with hardy perennials such as lupine, peonies, and daisies. Colors are bright. Bees buzz happily from peonies to daisies to the purple butterfly bush.

When they moved to the country, Lin began quilting, spending nine months on her first quilt, a sampler. Quilting and gardening take time. For Lin, the mystery of both lies in not knowing exactly how colors will look together until a project is finished. She says, "The surprises are always exciting! If the colors don't work in the garden, the plants can be moved. A quilt can be cut up and changed. You can add or take away or move pieces, or you can embellish and change everything."

Lin loves the unpredictability of plants. She finds inspiration in the way they grow, the relationship between flowers and leaves, and the color combinations within a single plant. Although black is absent in the garden, Lin uses it freely in her quilts to ground and intensify the colors, as soil does in the garden. "Black is brilliant," she says. When the camera lens focuses on a flower, notice how the background becomes blurred color. You can simulate this variation in the depth of field when you are choosing fabrics for a quilt.

Summertime brings friends into the side garden for an evening of Shakespeare among the hawthorns, honeysuckle, wisteria, and wild-rose hedges. In the fragrant shade, an old tool shed borders the area where the plays are staged. Ferns and other plants live in an old wheelbarrow and clay pots, which surround the brick courtyard. Moss grows on the old wood, creating a forest mood. Containers with ferns and other forest plants are tucked around the shrubs. Even though the home is old, the new garden has freed the structure from confinement. The old and new form a unique environment.

Tip

When designing a new part of your garden or planting a tree or shrub, estimate how it will look from different angles and from inside your house through the windows. Consider the height and width as well as color, texture, and adaptability to the soil and climate.

Buttercups in My Garden

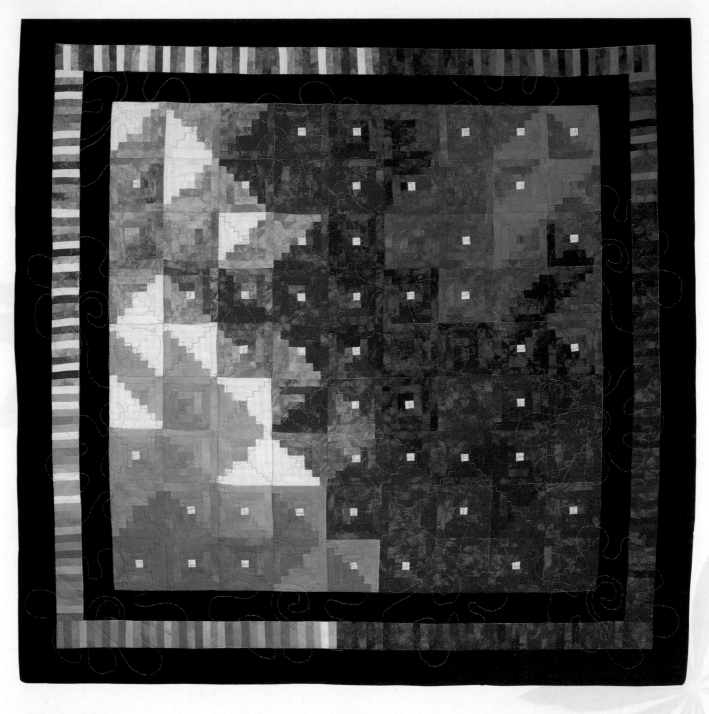

LIN PATTERSON
44" x 44"

Small Log Cabin blocks (3 ½" square) in a meadow of colors represent Lin's entire garden and allow her to play with color. Yellow buttercups that grow wild in the meadow appear as the centers of many of the blocks. To make the quilt, Lin hand-dyed 18 fat quarters in the primary and secondary hues of the color wheel. (This was enough fabric to complete the blocks and border.) She used Procion dyes; turquoise, lemon yellow, and raspberry yield the bright colors.

BUTTERCUPS IN MY GARDEN

Materials

- 4 ½ yards of fabric for dyeing, or fat quarters in the following colors: blue, blue-violet, violet, pink-violet, pink, pink-red, red, red-orange, orange, yellow-orange, yellow, yellow-green, green, blue-green
- Procion dyes in turquoise, lemon yellow, and raspberry (Fabric will be dyed according to Procion instructions in the colors above. See Sources, page 143.) Note that if you dye your own fabrics, colors (and blocks) may not come out exactly like Lin's.
- 1 yard black for first and third border and binding
- 2 yards for backing
- 48" x 48" batting

Cutting

Hand-dyed fabrics: Cut the fat quarters into 1" x 22" strips for the Log Cabin blocks and pieced border. Refer to the cutting chart to the right for the piece sizes.

Black: Cut nine 2 ½"-wide strips for the first and third borders.

For the first border, cut two 32" top and bottom strips and two 36" side strips.

For the third border, cut two 40" top and bottom strips. Piece remaining strips end-to-end, and cut two 44" side strips. Cut five 2"-wide strips and piece end-to-end for binding.

Instructions

1. Make blocks in sets of five. In each set, make three using buttercup yellow centers and two using centers of the first strip color.

2. Lay the fabrics out in the following order: blue, violet, pink, red, orange, yellow, and green. Because the fabric is hand-dyed, some will contain two of the neighboring colors such as red-orange and orange. Make the sets of blocks from the colors that lie next to each other, such as blue and violet or orange and yellow.

3. Make combinations equal to 14 sets of five blocks each (70 blocks total) in blue, blue-violet, violet, pink-violet, pink, pink-red, red, red-orange, orange, yellow-orange, yellow, yellow-green, green, and blue-green. After arranging the first blocks, check what colors may be needed to complete the design.

4. Make two more sets, and one additional block to fill in the pattern.

5. Use remaining strips in the pieced border.

Log Cabin Blocks

All strips are cut 1" wide.

Cutting Chart	
STRIP	**LENGTH**
1 & 2	1"
3 & 4	1 ½"
5 & 6	2"
7 & 8	2 ½"
9 & 10	3"
11 & 12	3 ½"
13	4"

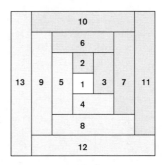

3 ½" finished

1. The length of each strip in the Log Cabin block is indicated in the chart. Trim the strips as you sew or, for greater accuracy, precut them to the lengths noted. With so many seams, it is especially important that stitching be precise; make sure to sew an accurate ¼" seam.

2. Join pieces 1 and 2, right sides together. Chain several together as shown below. Then clip the blocks apart and press toward 1.

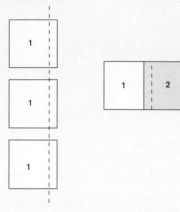

3. Place the 1-2 units, right sides together, atop piece 3, right sides together, as shown. Stitch, then cut units apart. Press toward 3.

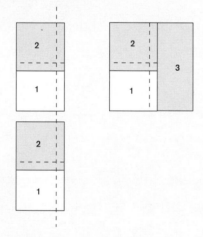

4. Add above unit to piece 4 and repeat step 3. Continue until you have finished the block. It will be 4" square (3½" square when finished).

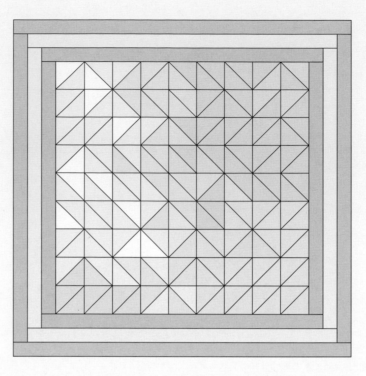

5. Arrange the blocks, referring to the photograph and illustration.

6. Stitch the blocks together into rows. Join row 1 to row 2, etc.

7. Add the first border to the sides of the quilt, then to the top and bottom.

8. For the pieced border, organize the strips in colors as in the blocks. You will need a total of 300 rectangles, each 1" x 2½". Refer to the photograph for the arrangement. For the side borders, stitch together 71 pieces; sew to the quilt. For the top and bottom borders, stitch together 79 pieces; sew to the quilt.

9. Add the third border to the sides of the quilt, then to the top and bottom.

10. For the machine-quilting in the Log Cabin blocks, Lin followed the piecing lines as shown. She stippled in the block borders, creating a denser pattern. Gold metallic thread creates a meandering pattern over the quilt.

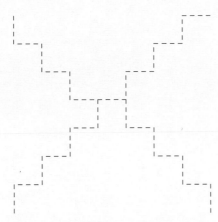

Outline quilting pattern for Log Cabin blocks

Curved line quilting pattern for border areas

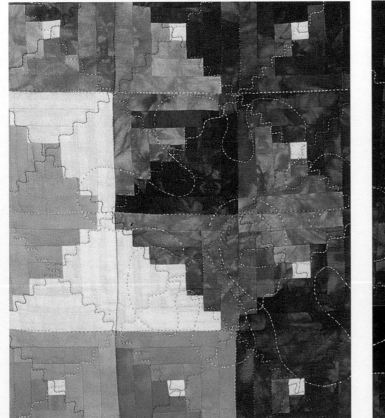

SARINA MEYER DE FEŸTER

Axel, The Netherlands

Garden Designer and Colorist

S arina was born on The Netherlands farm where she and her husband live in the original farmhouse. Over the years, working eight to nine hours a day during the gardening months, she has created a garden that has been featured in books and magazines. In the summer, Sarina leads tours through the garden and teaches classes, sharing her talents as a garden designer.

In 1980, with the help of a landscape architect, Sarina mapped out her garden, aiming for symmetry in the overall plan but with beds full of surprises. The drive was rerouted and lined with shade trees that create a buffer at the edge of the property. (It is the custom in The Netherlands to plant a tree when a daughter is born. Her family planted many trees.) Near the front entry, the beds were planted in shades of green, with well-trimmed topiaries. There is a layered feeling here, with unique shapes and surprising shades of green.

Colors in the garden have been planned meticulously, starting with yellow in the spring, followed by pink and then blue as spring progresses into summer. Fall brings the asters blending with late-blooming roses. Sarina also plants many medicinal and culinary herbs.

"Chicky Chick" is an old Dutch tuftbeard chicken that rules the garden. She wandered around, watching us, as we visited the garden.

An orchard with plum, cherry, and walnut trees emits a fragrance that keeps flies away in summer. Hedges outline an herb garden on the side of the house. A protective barrier against cold nights, the short hedges create a container-like feeling for the many herbs that are planted here.

Herbal fragrances draw you into the maze of hedges. Before planting, Sarina researches the medicinal and cosmetic uses of her plants. The oils in bright pink blooming roses, for example, are useful in rose water for cleaning the skin. Lavender, rosemary, sage, dill, and marjoram all have special culinary uses. The brick pathways draw you around the garden vignettes.

Although they require care, especially trimming and shaping, topiaries provide interesting shapes in the garden. For centuries European gardens have included topiaries. Sarina's are well-planned to add structure. Within the garden beds are wild plants and flowers, which interrupt the symmetry of the topiary shapes.

Sarina cultivates many plants in pairs. A clematis, for example, planted in a mugo pine creates the illusion of purple flowers in the evergreens. Roses and honeysuckle are planted together—an inviting fragrance when exploring the garden!

In this country setting 160 different roses flourish. Old roses around a bench invite a visitor to sit and enjoy the garden scene. A single rose bush cascades across the railing on the bridge at the pond. Another climbs a trellis. All bloom profusely and last from spring until early winter.

Sarina loves green. Lime, apple, sage, grass, moss, olive, spruce, and more—all combine into a serene backdrop for the color in the garden. Greens refresh the eye while blending naturally with the flower colors. When the flowers are finished blooming, green remains a neutral backdrop in this lively setting.

Sarina's garden is filled with all shades of blue and yellow. She chooses to use many fabrics from the The Netherlands that have a traditional Dutch look. Sarina used blue and yellow fabrics from The Netherlands in her quilt for this book. You might see this same style of design on pottery or in linens.

Near the house two formal beds filled with blue flowers (and a few yellow ones) flank a grassy area. Blue—from true blue to blue-violet—can be pale, cloudy, bright, and vibrant. Within these wildflowers, the variety of scale moves your eye through the beds. Insects, such as bumblebees, find a home in the lush garden.

Across a grassy area, yellow and white plantings surround a pond, drawing the eye to the color. Wisteria and roses drape the bridge. Grasses along the edge are home to dragonflies. Birds, fish, and frogs live among the pond lilies, which open in the late day sun, and close at night. Sarina has taken a large garden setting and created unique environments within each area.

Tip When asked for a gardening tip, Sarina advised, "Plant for the leaves. You have leaves from April to November but flowers for only six to eight weeks." In other words, showcase the differences in color and texture in the leaves of your plants. Sarina also plants in pairs—clematis in a mugo pine, for example, or honeysuckle and rose vines together.

Yellow and Blue

SARINA MEYER DE FEYTER
104" x 105 ½"

Flying Geese are set in rows, with blue and yellow Dutch print fabric between. Sashed in deep blue, the quilt is representative of the colors in The Netherlands and of the migrating geese that fly over the country in the fall and spring. On her property Sarina has both blue and yellow gardens, and some of the flowers mix beautifully in a third garden. Sarina used a scrap palette in the Flying Geese, personalizing the quilt. She hand-pieced and hand-quilted the design for her niece, whose favorite colors are yellow and blue. Her niece can't have a cat, so she featured cat fabric in several of the Geese units.

🐦 YELLOW AND BLUE

🐦 Materials

Refer to the illustration for fabric placement.

- A and E: a variety of prints totaling 4 1/2 yards
- B: 4 1/4 yards
- C, G, H, and binding: 2 1/2 yards
- D and F: 4 yards if cut crosswise, 5 1/2 yards if cut lengthwise without seams
- 108" x 110" batting

🐦 Cutting

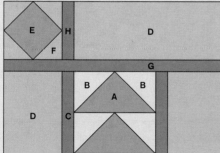

Various Prints:

For Flying Geese (A), cut nineteen 7 1/2 "-wide strips. Cut into 182 rectangles, each 4" x 7 1/2 ".

For corner squares (E), cut four 4 1/8" squares.

Fabric B:

For background for Flying Geese (B), cut thirty-seven 4"-wide strips. Cut into 364 squares, each 4" x 4".

Fabric C, G, H, and binding:

For vertical narrow sashing strips (C), cut thirty-three 1 1/2"-wide strips. Piece together end-to-end, and cut 14 lengths, each 91 1/2".

For horizontal narrow sashing strips (G), cut six 1 1/2"-wide strips. Piece together end-to-end, and cut two 105 1/2" lengths.

For corner narrow sashing strips (H), cut four 1 1/2" x 5 3/4" rectangles.

For binding, cut eleven 2"-wide strips and piece together end-to-end.

Fabric D and F:

For wide sashing strips (D), cutting directions differ depending on whether you cut with the crosswise or lengthwise grain. If crosswise: cut into nineteen 5 3/4"-wide strips. Piece together end-to-end, and cut into eight 91 1/2" lengths. For the top and bottom border, cut five 5 3/4"-wide strips; piece together end-to-end and cut into two 93" lengths. If cutting lengthwise, cut eight 91 1/2" lengths. For the top and bottom border cut two 93" lengths.

For corner triangles (F), cut eight 3 7/8" squares; cut each in half diagonally.

🐦 Instructions

1. To make the Flying Geese units, fold the background squares (B) in half diagonally and press. Place atop Flying Geese rectangle (A) with the fold positioned as shown. Stitch on the fold. Trim seam allowance 1/4" beyond the stitching line. Press. Repeat for the other side as shown. Make 182.

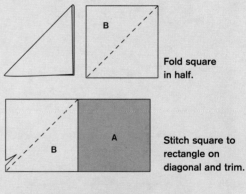

Fold square in half.

Stitch square to rectangle on diagonal and trim.

Press.

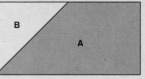

Repeat for other side.

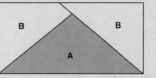

Make 182.

2. Arrange 26 Flying Geese in seven rows and stitch together. Press.

3. Stitch sashing strips and rows of Flying Geese together, as shown.

4. Add G to the top and bottom of the quilt.

5. Make four corners by stitching two triangles (F) to opposite sides of the square (E), then stitching the other two triangles (F) in place. Trim to 5 $^3/_4$ " square.

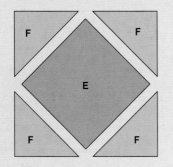

6. For the top border, stitch a short narrow sashing strip (H) to each end of a print border strip, then add the corner square (EF) to each end. Add to the top and bottom of the quilt.

7. Sarina hand-quilted the quilt following the outlines in the Flying Geese units and the sashing lines. In the print panels, she stitched 1"-wide diagonal lines at a 45° angle.

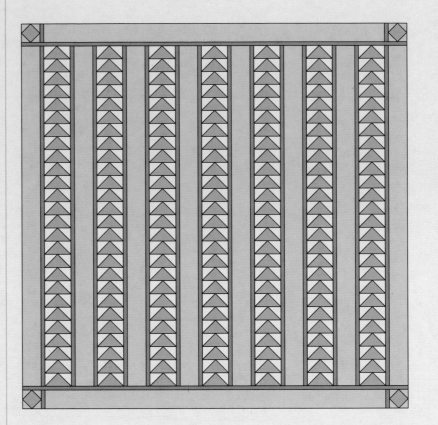

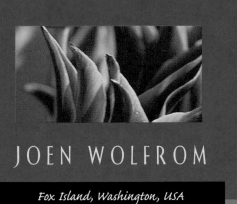

JOEN WOLFROM
Fox Island, Washington, USA

An Island Garden in the Puget Sound

In 1973, soon after she and her husband built their Northwest home, Joen began gardening. She planted over 100 rhododendrons, spring bulbs, and flowering ornamental trees for color in the spring. In the summer the yard fell to a quiet green, reflecting the serenity of the tall fir trees, the nearby mountains, and the waters of Puget Sound. Being surrounded by such great natural beauty has subtly influenced Joen's quilts over the years.

In 1993 gardening changed for Joen. Devastated by the death of her cousin, she found consolation in the garden. Having her hands in the soil renewed her spirit. She began to explore the potential in her yard. Envisioning the garden areas as individual rooms, she began planning each "garden room" in her mind. Naively, she thought her plan would be complete within five years. Happily, it has become a life-long endeavor.

In her second "Mother-Earth period," as she calls it, she discovered the value of perennials. Some of the garden rooms are filled with them. Finding unique plants to nestle here and there and watching them survive and bloom is most rewarding. She visualizes each room in her mind before creating it, much as you visualize a quilt before making it.

This author-quilter has written a number of books relating to color, light, and quilt design. Playing with colors—experimenting with the blends, values, boldness or subtlety, color combinations, and temperature—is the challenge that she embraces. She plays with color ideas in both quilting and gardening.

Ideas generated in this lush garden setting find their way into Joen's quilts. In fabric she plays with illusions of light—luster, luminosity, shadows, highlights, opalescence, iridescence—depth, and transparency. This stretches her mind and gives this artist great pleasure.

In her spring garden Joen is surrounded by tulips and other bulbs that herald the arrival of the season in the Northwest. So many varieties of tulips exist, walking along the paths is like leafing through a bulb catalogue. Pointed "Elegant Ladies" grow next to the "Ballade" tulips; around the corner are the regal "Emperors." Joen blends colors in the plantings much as she would in a quilt.

In this rural area, the garden is as informal as the setting. Giant trees and the wide expanse of water in the distance are a backdrop for the garden rooms that Joen creates. Around the pond, layered mossy rocks contribute to the serenity of the Japanese "garden room" that her husband is working on. A secret garden is also part of the plan, with a "room" on the bluff above the water, planted with a rainbow of colors for spring and summer viewing.

Ornamental flowering trees add fragrance as well as beauty to this island setting. They provide the perfect skeleton for a small, informal garden. In the white garden a bleeding heart blooms under a flowering cherry tree and white-flowering ground cover cascades over a garden wall. Joen prefers to be in the garden during the sunny days of spring, summer, and fall when the garden is ablaze with living color. She is happiest quilting in the dreary months of winter.

Being involved in the garden and surrounded by Puget Sound, a mountain range, islands, and beautiful countryside has inspired Joen to create landscape quilts. Now she wants to make quilts that are influenced by nature in a close-up state. You can see this influence in the photos. You want to touch the flowers, know them personally.

In the backyard is an abandoned tree fort that Joen's children used to play in. Overgrown with vines, it is a great hideout for future grandchildren.

Learning that a garden is a living, breathing thing, never quite finished, is comforting to this busy quilt artist. There is always something to change—add or take away—even after she thinks it is complete. "I love gardening because it's a creative adventure that never stops offering surprises, joy, and healthy exercise," she says. This creative adventure gives Joen a chance to work spontaneously. She lets the garden or the quilt design guide her to its outcome. For both endeavors, she brainstorms design ideas. She makes a skeletal plan, including as many of her design goals as appear feasible. She figures out which technique best suits her needs, and then determines the overall color plan.

Rhododendrons planted years ago provide a backdrop in the garden for smaller shrubs and perennials. The interplay of color values in the blossoms makes a quilt in itself. Joen's garden serves as a natural palette for this quilter, gardener, and author. Spring is glorious in Joen's garden.

Spring is Sprung

JOEN WOLFROM
21 1/4" x 28"

April in the Northwest is tulip season, when "Spring is Sprung." Joen captures the beauty of a single tulip using a curved piecing technique that she developed several years ago. You are sure to enjoy learning Joen's method as you stitch this simple design. Colors are handled much like those in a photograph that has been taken with a short depth of field—crisp foreground, soft background. The muted colors in the hand-dyed fabric are a perfect foil for the red tulip. Notice the variety of greens used in the foliage.

SPRING IS SPRUNG

Materials

- 1 1/4 yards total of reds, red-orange, and red-violet for the tulip, border, and binding
- 1/2 yard purple for border, piecing, and binding
- 1/2 yard total of darker and brighter greens for foliage
- 1/2 yard each of the pale versions of two color groups for the background
- 3/4 yard for backing
- Chalk pencil
- Plastic-coated freezer paper
- 24" x 33" batting

Cutting

The pattern is divided into three sections. Enlarge each section on page 69 by 265%, so the entire design measures 18 3/4" x 25 3/4" when assembled. Trace the enlarged patterns onto the uncoated side of freezer paper, transferring all markings. Using colored pencils, note color choices. Or, tape scraps of fabric to the pieces.

Cut apart pattern sections all at once or one piece at a time. By cutting the pattern apart one piece at a time, you can individually choose all of the fabrics.

Position the pattern piece, coated side down, atop the fabric, which is right side up. Press to secure. Cut a scant 1/4" beyond the paper.

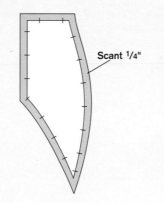

Scant 1/4"

Using a chalk pencil, transfer hash marks and also mark where seams intersect (for aligning pattern pieces). Lay the enlarged pattern on a table and place the cut piece on its appropriate space. This method keeps you organized.

Borders

Piece the borders at a 45° angle on the sides, placing red at the top and top sides, and purple on the bottom sides and bottom. From red, cut one 2" x 28" piece for top border, one 2" x 17" piece for top left side border, and 2" x 29" piece for one top right side border. From purple, cut one 2" x 28" piece for the bottom border, one 2" x 25 1/2" piece for the bottom left side border, and one 2" x 10" piece for the bottom right side. These measurements allow for mitered corners. The binding will be cut the same lengths and pieced on the sides.

Instructions

1. The pieces in the pattern are numbered in piecing order starting in section one. You may find another sequence that you feel will work better for you. (There isn't just one way to complete the tulip quilt.)

2. All of the curves in this pattern are gentle. On the concave pieces, clip into the seam allowance only slightly. Be consistent in the length of the cuts and the distances between them to create smooth curves. Remove freezer paper before stitching pieces together.

3. Hash marks have been added for you to use as matching points. (Stitch only to the end of the pattern piece, not through the seam allowance.) Pin together the end points at the seam allowance. Then match up the hash marks and pin. Stitch the seam, removing pins to avoid stitching over them.

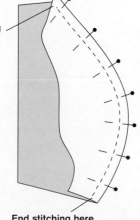

Start stitching here.

End stitching here.

There will be places where three points come together. Match up the end points, pushing the other seam allowance aside. (It is easier than you think.) Think of it as a puzzle, one piece at a time. Follow the piecing charts below:

Section 1

Sew 1 to 2, then add 3.

Sew to 4, then add 5.

Sew 6 to 7, then add 8.

Sew to 1–5 unit, then add 9.

Section 2

Sew 1 to 2.

Sew 3 to 4, then add to 1–2 unit.

Sew 5 to 6, then add 1–4 unit.

Sew 7 to 8, then add to 1–6 unit; add 9. Sew 10 to 11 to 12 to 13, then add to 1–9 unit.

Section 3

Sew 2 to 3. Add 1, then add 4 and sew to 5; add 6.

Sew 7 to 8, then sew 1–5 unit to 7–8 unit. Add 9, then add 10 to intersection.

Sew 11 to 12, then add to 1–10 unit.

Sew 13 to 14, then add to 1–12 unit.

Add 15 to all.

4. Finish the three sections and join them together. There is no right or wrong direction to press the seams. If you want the tulip to come to the surface more, press the outer edges toward the tulip. The same is true with the leaves if you want them to stand out. If necessary, trim the edges to measure 19 $\frac{1}{4}$" x 26 $\frac{1}{4}$" including seam allowances. Stay-stitch $\frac{1}{4}$" inside the edge to stabilize the top.

5. Make the side borders, using the photo and the illustration as guides. Lay the purple and red pieces at 90° angles. Mark a 45° angle. Stitch, trim seams, and press open to create each side border.

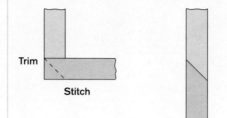

Trim

Stitch

6. To miter the corners, stitch each of the borders on the edges of the quilt, starting and stopping $\frac{1}{4}$" from each quilt edge. Press seams toward the border. Fold one border strip under so that it meets the edge of the adjoining border and forms a 45° angle. Press the fold, turn the quilt over, open the fold, and stitch along the

fold line toward the outside point. Trim the excess to a $\frac{1}{4}$" seam allowance and press the seam open.

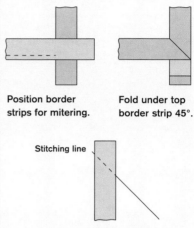

Position border strips for mitering.

Fold under top border strip 45°.

Stitching line

Open fold and stitch.

7. Piece the purple and red strips for the side binding and match the seams to the seams on the border. Bind the quilt.

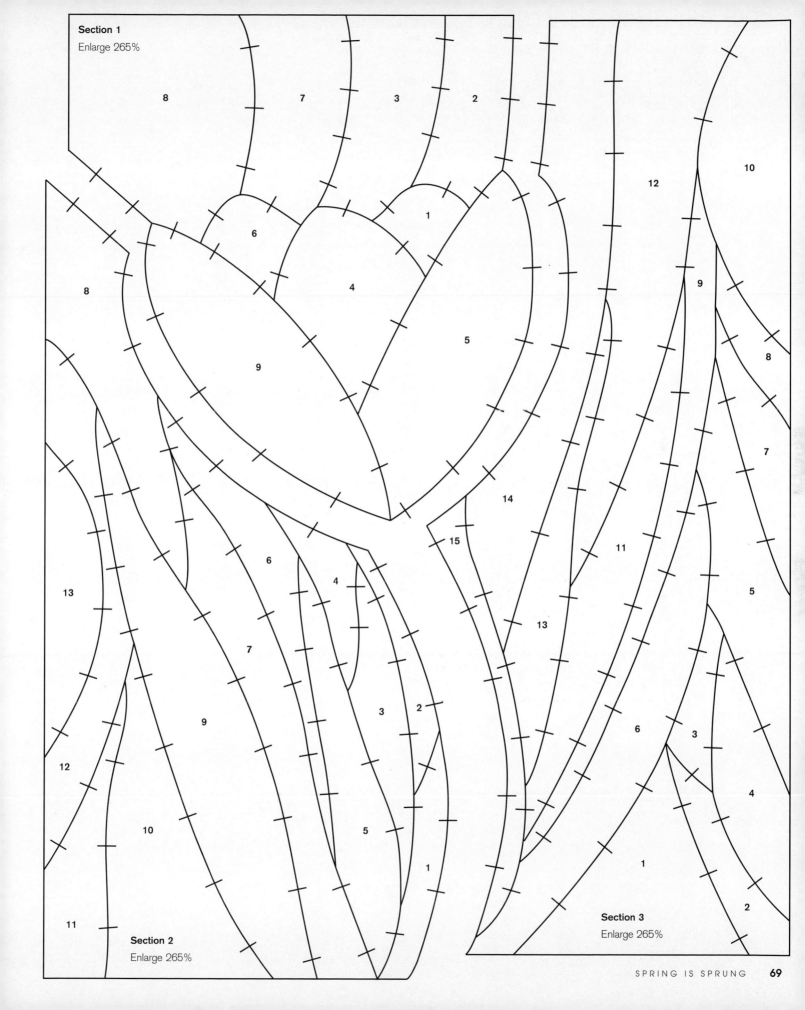

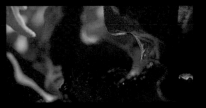

Sisters, Oregon, USA

A Garden Room Inside & Out

This energetic post-Olympic skier focuses her energy on her home, garden, and quilting, creating a one-of-a-kind setting in rural Central Oregon. Sherry claims to have had the world's greatest grandmother, who was a wonderful cook, hand sewer, and gardener. She can remember going as a five-year-old with her grandmother to the church basement quilting bees. Yet, Sherry felt these "repressed genes" didn't begin to grow within her for another 30 years. Then, at the age of 35, she suddenly had the interest and motivation to garden, cook, and quilt.

Sherry and her husband, Rich, added a 450 foot greenhouse to one of their out buildings, which Sherry proceeded to turn into a "garden room" complete with trompe l'oeil painting on the wall. This European-style setting houses the plants Sherry starts, keeping them growing during the cold Central Oregon springs (that seem like a continuous "frost alert"). Most spring evenings, the Morrises entertain friends for dinner in their garden room: a conservatory filled with color, greenery, and tiny white lights.

Sherry's creativity flows when she's in her garden room. In early spring, she meticulously plans and plants within moss-covered containers. She scours flea markets, yard sales, and antique shops for interesting items that could be pots for her many planting ideas. She selects mostly pink and purple flowering plants, coupling them with interesting foliage that highlights her gray house. Once the containers are filled, Sherry nurtures the plants with a daily dose of water-soluble fertilizer until they can live outside.

Based on a suggestion that she needed lawn chairs, Sherry cut out the seats from two wooden folding chairs. She replaced them with chicken wire, then added moss and planted grass and ivy. Now she has her "lawn chairs." Sherry enjoys the process of creativity. She likes working on projects, but once they are finished she is ready to start another. The same is true whether she is decorating her house or designing a quilt.

Envision a European garden plaza and you will be stepping into Sherry and Rich's wrought-iron fenced-in garden. Stone corners and arches divide the garden into spaces filled with flowers. Inviting benches lure visitors to sit among the living wreaths, with their tiny pink blossoms, and the cascading petunias, to enjoy the courtyard.

Sherry got the idea for the wrought-iron fence when she took a trip to France with friends. Deer eat breakfast, lunch, and dinner in most people's gardens, but here the attractive fence keeps the deer out while providing a wonderful view for the couple. One caution Sherry mentions is that a friend tried the same thing but didn't put the iron posts close enough together and the deer were able to stick their heads through the fence and nibble.

Within the fence are raised beds filled with several varieties of ornamental cabbage, day lilies, tall yellow hollyhocks, and scented geraniums. The colors of the cabbage alone, with all the shades of green and pink, are inspiration for a winter quilt.

During summer days when everything has been planted, Sherry sits in the courtyard reading or planning her next garden project. Sherry created a fountain from a large terra-cotta pot. She sank miniature cattails and grasses into river rock within the pot, letting the water circulate from the pot to flow down to the rocks and back up again. You would never know there was a child's swimming pool sunk below the surface to create this effect.

Tip   Container gardening is not just for people with limited space. Containers fill empty spaces, are portable, and decorate a porch or deck—or, if you are like Sherry and don't like weeds—container gardening is the perfect solution for a green thumb. Be sure to put gravel or broken clay pots in the bottom of each container. If it is a very deep container, packing peanuts (the white stuff) can be used halfway up before adding potting soil. You will also be able to lift it if you want to move the pot. Purchase good quality potting soil. If you purchase plants in containers, check that they are not root bound. If so, simply massage the roots and remove any excess.

Plan the container gardens based on plant height, color, and texture to maximize your efforts. Water regularly, making sure the containers don't dry out in the hot summer months. Fertilize regularly or use water-soluble fertilizer daily.

Redwork Path

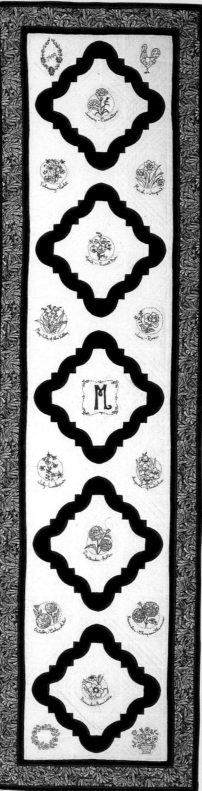

SHERRY MORRIS
26 1/2" x 98 1/2"

Intrigued by the structure of ironwork, Sherry chose to use the Drunkard's Path quilt block in black and white for her quilt. She had been wanting a long, narrow quilt to put in her stairwell, so the quilt was designed to fit that space. Sherry has a collection of antique redwork quilts and wanted to put redwork in this quilt. She chose flower transfers that represent the twelve months of the year from an "Aunt Martha's" hot-iron transfer book. Sherry has an extensive collection of redwork quilts, so it was only natural for her to choose red thread for the embroidery. She also included an "M" for Morris and a chicken motif, which is Sherry's signature mark.

REDWORK PATH

Materials

- 1 $^3/_4$ yards white for piecing
- 2 yards black for piecing, borders, and binding
- $^1/_2$ yard red for border inserts
- $^2/_3$ yard print for second border
- 3 yards backing
- Two skeins six-stranded red embroidery floss
- Aunt Martha's Flower-of-the-Month embroidery pattern (see Sources, page 143)
- Harriet Hargrave's *Curved Piecing à la Appliqué*, Drunkard's Path template (see Sources, page 143)
- Plastic-coated freezer paper
- Nylon invisible thread
- Fabric (basting) glue stick
- 31" x 103" batting

Cutting

From the white fabric, cut fifteen 3 $^1/_2$"-wide strips. Cut the strips into one hundred sixty 3 $^1/_2$" squares. Cut one 6 $^1/_2$"-wide strip, then cut the strip into five 6 $^1/_2$" squares.

From the black fabric, cut twelve 1"-wide strips. Cut two 18 $^1/_2$" and two 25 $^1/_2$" lengths from the strips. Piece the remaining black strips end-to-end and cut two 91" and two 98 $^1/_2$" lengths.

From the red fabric, cut twelve 1"-wide strips. Cut two 19 $^1/_2$" and two 25 $^1/_2$" lengths from the strips. Piece the remaining red strips end-to-end and cut two 91" and two 97 $^1/_2$" lengths.

From the print fabric, cut six 3 $^1/_2$" wide strips. Cut two 19 $^1/_2$" lengths from the strips. Piece the remaining strips end-to-end and cut two 97 $^1/_2$" lengths.

Instructions

1. Trace and cut 100 Drunkard's Path templates (page 81) on the paper-side of the freezer paper. Press the shiny side of the freezer-paper templates on the back side of the black fabric, matching grain lines on the straight edges. Space templates to allow a $^3/_{16}$" seam on the curved edge. The $^1/_4$" seam allowance is included on the straight edges of the template. Cut the shapes, adding a $^3/_{16}$" seam allowance around the curved edge.

Add a $^3/_{16}$" seam allowance.

2. Apply basting glue to the paper on the curved edge and gently roll the seam allowance onto the freezer paper with the glue on it.

3. Thread the sewing machine with the invisible nylon thread, using a lightweight thread in the bobbin. Set the machine to a blind hem stitch or a very narrow and long zigzag stitch. Practice the stitch on a scrap to make adjustments before you start. You may need to tighten the bobbin tension to get an even stitch.

4. Place the black pieces on top of the white 3 $^1/_2$" squares, matching the straight edges in a corner. Pin in place. Stitch around the curve. Pull away the freezer paper. Turn the block to the wrong side and trim away the white background fabric under the black to within $^1/_4$" of the seam line.

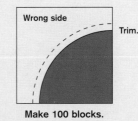
Make 100 blocks.

5. Stitch four Drunkard's Path squares together and stitch to each side of a 6 1/2" white square. Stitch the rest of the squares in rows and stitch rows on either side of the center.

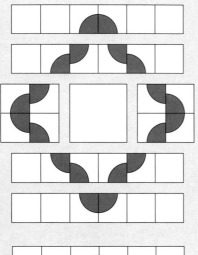

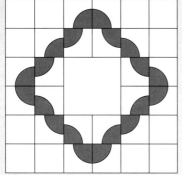

6. Following the manufacturer's instructions, transfer the embroidery designs to the block centers.

7. Using two strands of embroidery floss, use an outline stitch to stitch the embroidery patterns.

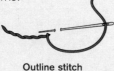

Outline stitch

8. Join the blocks together. Transfer and stitch the remaining embroidery designs.

9. Using two strands of floss, use an outline stitch to embroider the outside and inside of the black design.

10. Add the first black borders top and bottom, then the sides. Press toward the black border. Press the red strips in half lengthwise, with the wrong sides together, and match the raw edges. Pin to the top and bottom of the quilt, then the sides. The corners will overlap.

11. Add the second (print) border, top and bottom, and then the sides. Press the seam toward the black border. With raw edges matching, pin the second set of red strips on the second border. Add the outer black borders, repeating the process. Press seams toward the black border.

12. Add a row of outline stitches where the first black border meets the white fabric. Sherry hand-quilted a one-inch crosshatch design diagonally across the quilt surface to highlight the ironwork-style design she created.

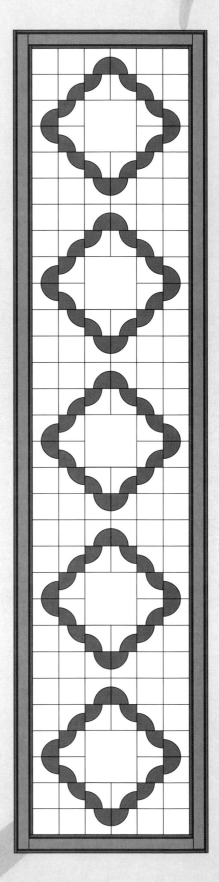

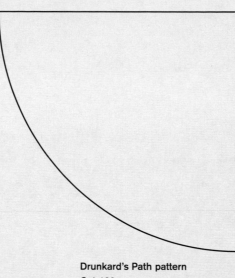

Drunkard's Path pattern
Cut 100.

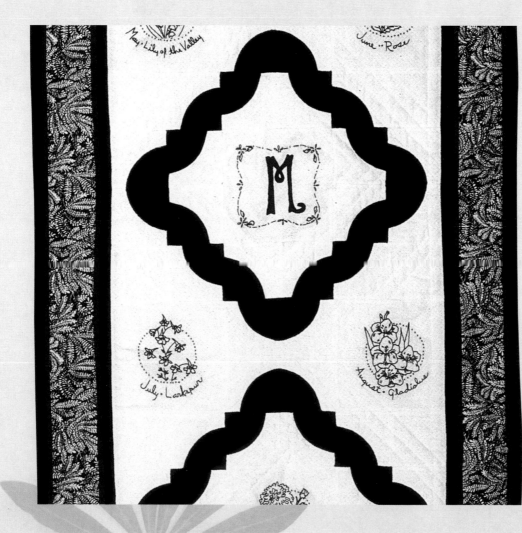

JINNY BEYER

Great Falls, Virginia, USA

Restored Plantation Garden

I n the 1970s, Jinny won a quilt contest sponsored by *Good Housekeeping* magazine—a victory that marked the beginning of her successful career. A quilter before she became a gardener, her eye for design and her attention to balance, contrast, repetition, and detail characteristic of her quilts and fabric designs are equally evident in the garden.

The first structure on a 2,000-acre plantation, this cabin was built around 1770. The original family probably lived in it while the main house was being built. Through the years it has served many purposes. In 1822, for example, it was a weaving house. Today it is Jinny's studio, a place to store fabric, plan her quilt conferences, and design quilts.

Over the years Jinny has created a perennial garden full of plants that do well in this Virginia setting. She pays close attention to what blooms when so there is constantly something in flower.

When we visited we were greeted by a downpour. Even with the spring shower, however, the garden was magical, as you can see from the water droplets on the flowers. Once in a while the sun peeked through the clouds and lit up the landscape.

Old-fashioned wood roses were probably some of the first flowers on this property. Field grasses provide a pastoral background for shrubbery, trees, and perennials. Open meadows, groves of trees, and small ponds inspire this quilter.

The pathway beside the cottage leads to rock steps at the front door where "Cat" awaits. The guardian of the garden, "Cat" leads us from one area to the next. Every time we turn a corner there is "Cat."

Lured by the sound of running water, we walk around the cottage and discover a small pond. Once there, the fragrance of mock orange blossoms envelopes us. The white flowers charm us. The large bush engulfing the edge of the pond, creates a setting one would expect to read about in a novel.

Hidden behind the mock orange, the statue of a woman watches over the pond. The empty bench is an invitation to sit and enjoy the intimate setting Jinny has created. Roses lean over the edge of the pond, dropping their petals into the water. Purple irises are a striking presence. It is easy to see that "Cat" might enjoy dreaming of catching fish here.

Jinny feels that quilting has influenced her gardening more than the other way around, making her aware of balance, color mixing, and continuity. For Jinny, gardening is relaxing. When she works hard on writing and designing, she takes a break every few hours to wander outside, pull weeds, dead-head roses, fertilize the plants, or watch the fish in the pond.

Jinny's perennial plants vary in height, shape, texture, and blooming time, to create a continuous treat for the eye and inspiration for her fabric designs. While the jewel tones in her fabrics are reminiscent of Persian rugs, the pastel combinations in the fabrics are those of a spring garden.

Nostalgic peonies with full pink faces are planted along the naturalistic grape arbor. When the peonies finish blooming, another flower will take their place, and in the fall grapes will hang from the vines, waiting to be harvested.

The irises are a study in color, contrast, and hue. Looking at the relationships in these flowers, we see how Jinny might come up with a palette for a line of fabric. We see that she is influenced by unexpected beauty found in the garden.

Cottage Basket

DESIGNED BY JINNY BEYER
CREATED BY CAROLE NICHOLAS
61" x 61"

Jinny is known for her unique border-prints, one of which inspired her traditional *Cottage Basket* quilt. The colors in her rain-spattered garden on the day we photographed remind us of the fabrics she chose for this quilt—soft pastels with a misty quality and splashes of pink and yellow. The quilt is a study in ways of incorporating stripes into the piecing process and the borders.

COTTAGE BASKET

Materials

- 6 1/2 yards soft border print for baskets, setting triangles, borders, binding, and backing
- 5/8 yard for background of the basket blocks
- 5/8 yard for inside triangles in the baskets (basket filler) and the second border
- 1/8 yard each of seven coordinating fabrics for the small triangles that suggest a handle on the baskets (light, medium, and dark values)
- Optional: 2" finished half-square-triangle paper for making D
- 65" x 65" batting

Cutting

Referring to page 95, make plastic templates for A, B, and F. The templates allow you to position the triangles atop the print for maximum effect before cutting.

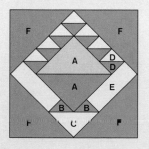

If working with one of Jinny's stripes, cut four 2-yard lengths of the wider border stripe and four 60" lengths of the narrow border stripe. Reserve these for the border of the quilt.

Border Print

For Basket (A), place template A on the border print to determine where you want to focus the basket. Trace around the template. Cut out nine identical pieces.

For Base of Basket (B), place template B on the border print to determine placement, and cut 18 base triangles.

For Setting Triangles (F), place template F on the border print and determine where you want to focus the design. Remember that the 90° corners will meet up with three others to create another block design. (Refer to the photograph of the quilt.) Trace around the template and cut a total of 36 triangles.

Basket Filler Print

Use template A, or cut five 6 7/8" squares, then cut each in half diagonally (you will use nine of the ten pieces). Use remaining fabric for the second border.

Background Fabric

For C, cut five 4 7/8" squares, then cut each in half diagonally.

For D, use triangle paper or cut three 2 7/8"-wide strips. Cut into thirty-two 2 7/8" squares, then cut each in half diagonally.

For E, cut three 2 1/2"-wide strips. From these cut eighteen 6 1/2" rectangles.

Assorted Light, Medium, and Dark Fabrics

For D, use triangle paper or cut thirty-two 2 7/8" squares, then cut each in half diagonally.

Instructions

Block

1. Use half-square paper, or stitch D background triangle to D print triangle, right sides together, creating a square. Press toward the darker fabric; trim corners. Make 63.

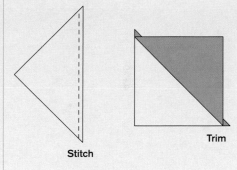

2. Stitch a border-print triangle (A) to a basket-filler triangle (A), creating a square. Press toward border print. Make nine.

3. Arrange the D blocks in stacks of nine. Stitch together three blocks for right side of A. Stitch together four blocks for the left side of A.

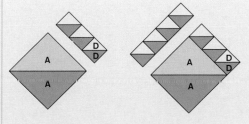

Add the three-block row to the A block; press toward A. Then add the four-block row and press toward A.

4. Stitch the B triangles to the left and right sides of 18 E rectangles, creating mirror images. Stitch to the block, referring to the block illustration. Press toward B/E. Then, stitch a C triangle to the bottom of the block. Press toward C.

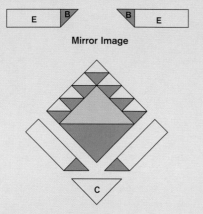

Mirror Image

5. Stitch an F triangle to each side of the block. Press toward F.

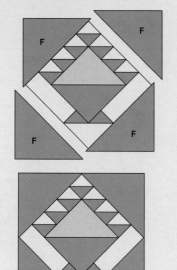

6. Join blocks together in three rows of three blocks each. Join rows together.

Borders

For adding the borders, we will use Jinny Beyer's instructions for framing a square or block using border print fabrics.

1. Cut the narrower border into $1^1/2$"-wide strips. Place a strip of the border print across the middle of the quilt, centering the motif from the border in the exact center of the piece. (Measuring across the middle as opposed to the edges is more accurate and will keep the quilt from "ruffling" at the edges.)

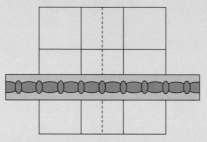

Align center of border motif with center of quilt.

2. Using a right-angle triangle or the 45° line on a ruler, mark the miter along the edges, making sure to add $1/4$" seam allowance. Cut along marked line.

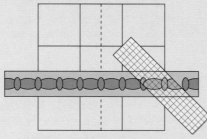

Mark a 45° angle with the ruler. Add $1/4$" for seam allowance.

3. Carefully pick up the mitered edge of the border strip and bring it over to the other end of the border strip at the opposite edge of the quilt, making sure that the design matches. (If you have centered a motif from the border print in the middle of the quilt, the designs should match at both edges.) Cut the second miter.

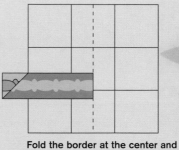

Fold the border at the center and cut the second miter.

4. Using the first mitered piece as a guide, cut three more identical pieces, making sure that the design on the border print is exactly the same on all four pieces.

5. Pin the mid-point of one of the border pieces to the edge of the quilt, centering it in the middle. Pin the corners next, then ease in any fullness, pinning carefully all along the edge. Stitch to $1/4$" from the end of each border and backstitch.

6. For the second border, cut six $2^1/2$"-wide strips. Piece together end-to-end. Cut into four 54" lengths. Add to quilt as above. To create the mitered corners, follow the instructions and illustrations for Joen Wolfrom's quilt on p. 68, Step 6.

7. Using the $6^1/2$" border strips, cut as in Steps 2–4 and add to quilt as above, mitering the corners.

8. This is the perfect design to quilt traditionally until you get to the border prints. Then follow the lines in the border prints, creating a relief design.

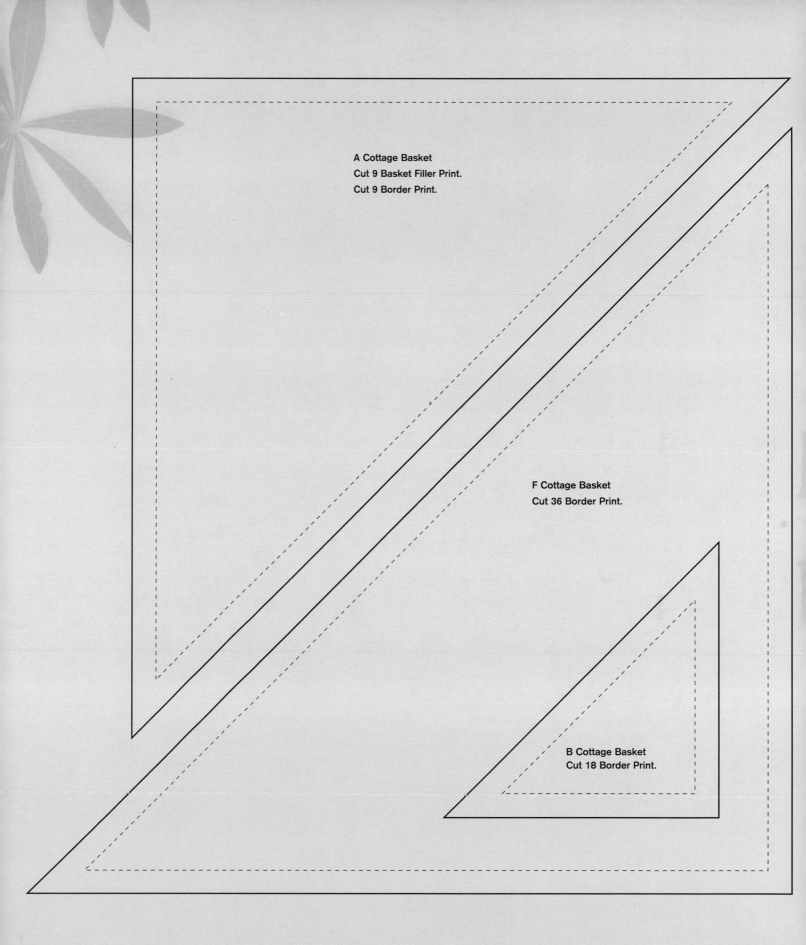

A Cottage Basket
Cut 9 Basket Filler Print.
Cut 9 Border Print.

F Cottage Basket
Cut 36 Border Print.

B Cottage Basket
Cut 18 Border Print.

JANE MARSHALL

Elmswell, England

Rose Cottage

Built in 1600, Rose Cottage is a quaint, flower-bedecked brick house in Suffolk County, England. Here Jane and her husband have nurtured the long-established garden, adding their own touches. On the brick patio, for example, containers of bright flowers sit atop and around a white iron table nestled beneath a window. Stenciling on the courtyard window resembles white lace curtains, enhancing the storybook charm of the setting.

A business copywriter, Jane finds quilting and gardening provide a welcome contrast to her work because they are practical, tactile pastimes. She loves making quilts for others and the challenge of creating designs that fit their personal styles. Quilting has definitely influenced her gardening. Many of the color ideas in the garden are the result of her experiences in quilting. Gardening has influenced her quilting, too, helping her see colors more readily in fabrics. Jane's aim is to turn her garden into a beautiful backdrop for photographing quilts.

Jane likes to accessorize her patio with movable pots of flowers. They give her the opportunity to fill bare spots or create vignettes in the garden. Container gardening enables her to easily explore combinations of color and shape.

 Lady's Bonnet, the Suffolk name for columbine, is prevalent at Rose Cottage, but roses are everywhere. Red and pink rose bushes cover the landscape in front of the house. The red rose, Ena Harkness, comes from one of the country's most famous rose-growing families. The pink rose is named for Queen Elizabeth. White New Dawn roses climb the wall of the old brick cottage and the archway into the back garden. They smell wonderful on a warm, summer evening. Through the archway into the back-yard, containers of flowers and greenery abound.

Mature vines create a trellis-like entrance to Jane's garden. White roses and a few pink blossoms fill the trellis, guiding the way to Jane's studio-office at the side of the house. Working here, Jane has a bird's-eye view of her garden. The green setting provides a serene environment for her studio-office.

For Jane, the repetitive nature of quilting and gardening is soothing after a day at work. She finds a strong sense of achievement in both. She also feels increasing pleasure in the fact that each is controlling you as much as you are controlling them. "I'm talking about happy, unexpected accidents," she says, "like self-seeding flowers—fabrics that kind of jump together even if you hadn't planned it that way—and a sense of not-quite-ordered chaos!" There is a freedom in gardening and quilting that comes from the enjoyment of the chaos and unpredictability.

Jane's taste in quilting spills into her garden. She prefers scrap quilting— creating works of art from bits and pieces. Her garden has a scrap-quilt look, with pots of flowers and bits and pieces of different plants combined into the whole. White acts as a light source in the garden; splashes here and there draw you around the setting.

Jane's quilting influences her gardening. She sees colors more easily in fabric than in nature, for example, and puts her color ideas from quilting to work in the garden. She plants bright orange marigolds among complementary blue flowers, and she cultivates pink roses with white ones to soften the stark green leaves and white petals of the dominant white bushes. Her motto, she says, is to "Try not to garden by the rules but by intuition. Just like I quilt, in fact."

Tip Jane says, "As a fundamentally lazy gardener with limited time, I love to garden as much as possible in containers. The containers do require watering more often. Apart from that, if something looks sick or dies you can just remove or replant the pot. The colors of the pots and their shapes enhance the arrangements and help get a good height variation. And you can change things 'round easily if you get bored."

Midsummer Madness

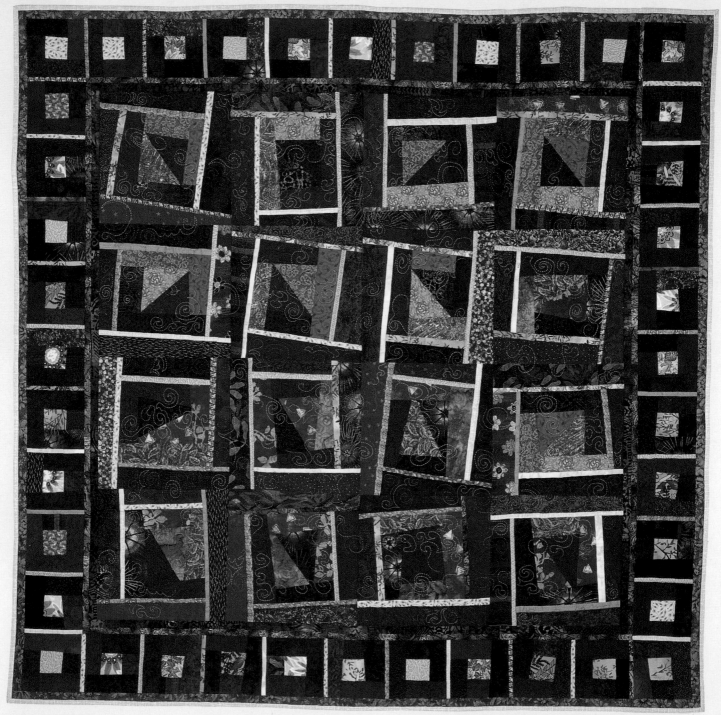

JANE MARSHALL
47" x 47"

Beneath the window of Rose Cottage, right under the name-plate, are two very old roses. The blossoms on these bush roses begin as red-orange buds. In full flower they turn a deep, velvety red, verging on red-violet. As the petals fade and fall, they change again to a nearly black purple. All this contrasts with the yellow-green of the leaves on the roses and the surrounding sedum, Lady's Bonnet (aquilegia) and Gerber daisies. Thus the palette for *Midsummer Madness* was born in Jane's mind.

For Jane, the fabrics precede the design. For this quilt, she experimented with block elements, coming up with this free-form design that verges on crazy-quilt style. The construction of the blocks resembles Log Cabin piecing. Assembled blocks are trimmed to uniform sizes. Yellow-green strips between them represent interlocking paths or the trellis Jane saw in the roses. Free-motion machine quilting carries out the theme of the roses and surrounding leaves.

MIDSUMMER MADNESS

Materials

A variety of abstract, geometric, and representational prints, in different scales, coupled with several batiks and hand-dyed fabrics:

- Scraps (larger than 7 1/2" square) or 1/4 yard cuts equal to 2 3/4 yards of orange, red-orange, orange-pink, red, red-violet, and purple fabrics
- 1 1/4 yards total of yellow-green prints, from very light to medium-dark for blocks, sashing, and binding
- 1/4 yard each of two dark olive greens for inner borders
- 1/4 yard of one olive green for the fourth border
- 2 1/4 yards of backing fabric
- 51" x 51" batting

Cutting

You will be making two sets of eight blocks. Make two copies of the pattern on page 107. For each set of eight blocks, cut eight 7 1/2" squares of different orange, red-orange, orange-pink, red, red-violet, and purple fabrics. Replace one or two of these squares with darker yellow-greens for more visual texture, if desired.

Layer the eight squares atop one another, right sides up, to make a neat stack. Place the pattern on top of the stacked squares and cut on the lines through all the layers.

For the first border, cut top and bottom strips 1" x 36 1/2", and two side strips 1" x 37 1/2".

For the second border, cut top and bottom strips 1" x 37 1/2", and two side strips 1" x 38 1/2".

For the fourth border, cut five strips 1"-wide strips. Piece end-to-end, and then cut top and bottom strips 46" long and two side strips 47" long.

Cut sashing as you work.

Instructions

1. Carefully separate the pieces for the centers of the block. Lay them out to form eight blocks in a pleasing color arrangement. Try not to use the same fabric twice in any one block.

2. Sew the pieces together in the numbered order, starting with pieces #1 and #2. You will find that the pieces don't match up precisely, but that doesn't matter.

Trim off excess fabric after each strip is sewn on. You will end up with a strangely shaped block, probably with a couple of pieces extending off the end.

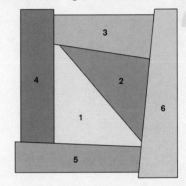

3. Trim the blocks. They can be square or rectangular, depending on your preference.

4. Cut fifteen varying 3/4"-wide to 1"-wide sashing strips from the yellow-green fabrics. Cut fifteen 2"-wide sashing strips of orange, red-orange, orange-pink, red, red-violet, and purple. (You may cut these as needed.)

Starting on the side of one block, add a yellow-green strip followed by a 2"-wide strip in the color of your choice. Press. Repeat on the remaining sides of the block. Press, but do not trim yet.

5. Join the strips to the remaining blocks in the same manner.

6. Using a ruler, square up each block to $9 \frac{1}{2}$" x $9 \frac{1}{2}$".

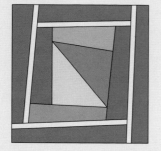

Add a yellow-green strip followed by a 2"-wide strip to each side of the block.

7. Arrange the blocks in a pleasing design, then join them into rows. Stitch the rows together.

8. Add the first border to the top and bottom, then to the sides.

9. Add the second border in the same manner.

The third border consists of pieced blocks. To begin assembly, cut two $1 \frac{7}{8}$"-wide strips from the lightest of the yellow-green fabrics. Then cut the strips into 40 "rough" squares.

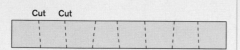

11. Using approximately 2"-wide strips of the darker red and purple fabrics used in the center blocks, add a single round of Log Cabin strips around each square. You will have 40 squares.

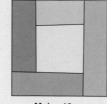

Make 40.

Trim 24 squares to $4 \frac{1}{4}$" x $4 \frac{1}{4}$". Trim 16 squares to $4 \frac{1}{4}$" x $4 \frac{1}{2}$". (Four of these will be mixed in on each side of the quilt to make the measurment come out right.)

12. For the top and bottom borders, arrange five $4 \frac{1}{4}$" squares with four $4 \frac{1}{4}$" x $4 \frac{1}{2}$" squares between (nine blocks total). Sew a $\frac{7}{8}$"-wide yellow-green strip between each block and on each end. Add to the quilt top and bottom. Repeat for the sides, adding $4 \frac{1}{4}$" blocks to each end for a total of 11 blocks in the unit. Omit the yellow-green strips at the ends of the strips. Join to the quilt top.

13. Add the fourth border to the top and bottom of the quilt, then to the sides.

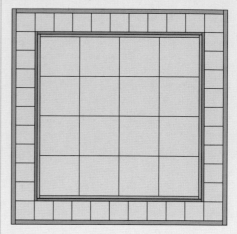

14. Jane finished her quilt using free-motion quilting, choosing threads that matched the colors in the quilt. To make the green areas stand out, she avoided quilting on the narrow strips and centers of the third border blocks. Her quilt designs are shown on page 107.

15. Bind the quilt.

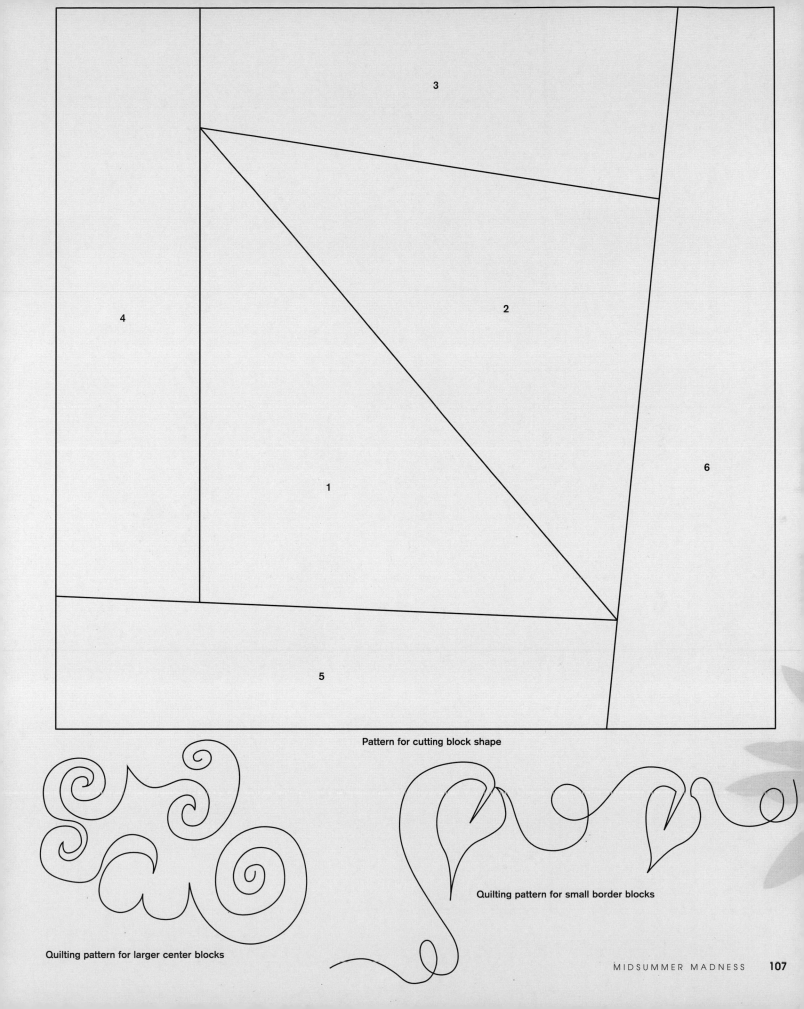

3

4

2

1

6

5

Pattern for cutting block shape

Quilting pattern for small border blocks

Quilting pattern for larger center blocks

BECKY GOLDSMITH

Sherman, Texas, USA

Drought Tolerant Texas Gardens

I n Sherman, Texas where appliqué artist Becky Goldsmith lives, flower gardens are a challenge because of the climate and the clay soil, which is only four- to ten-inches deep. Visiting Becky in October, we saw her efforts in full bloom, starting with sweet smelling abelia bushes in front of her white brick ranch house. Walter, the cat, sat on the brick wall, casually welcoming us to the garden.

Busy with her career and her family, Becky doesn't have a lot of gardening time. Nonetheless, it provides a welcome chance to relax. When asked about her choice in plantings, Becky says, "I'm a very competitive gardener, and I like my yard to look nice around the house." She loves visitors' reactions to her garden because hers is one of the few homes on her street with flowers in the yard.

Becky gardens because she loves the interplay of colors in her yard and the challenge of making her home and garden beautiful. "Gardening and quilting both give you results," she says, "something to show for your efforts."

Finding plants in addition to cactus that can withstand the heat in Sherman is a challenge. Texas bluebonnets, the state flower, are among the plants that thrive in high temperatures. They reseed themselves each year to brighten the spring landscape.

Butterflies moving from flower to flower add life and color to the setting.

Lantana also thrives in Sherman's hot, dry climate. Its vivid colors pull the eye through the flower beds. After blooming, the berry-like seed pods add texture to the garden. As the plants mature, seed pods form, and new shapes and colors change the garden setting with the Texas seasons.

Granite rocks found near the Oklahoma border enhance the sloping beds in front of the house. Becky's husband, Steve, a field biologist, encourages the cultivation of native plants from East Texas, such as grasses that grow well in the clay soil adding year-round texture and color. Through Steve, Becky has learned about the insects and other animals that live in her garden. Even grasshoppers are welcome in small doses. Their coloring repeats the hues in the grass, their natural habitat.

Becky became a gardener when she first got her own patch of dirt. Although she didn't pay much attention to the plants her mother tended, some of her mother's knowledge rubbed off on her. As a result, wherever she has lived she has cultivated plants. On her backyard patio, cacti in pots are joined in the fall by mums and pumpkins that provide seasonal color.

Becky enjoys both gardening and quilting because of the process. For her, hand appliqué is especially relaxing. "People often remark that hand appliquérs must be very patient people," she says, "and really the opposite is true. I'm so impatient that I can't sit still with nothing to work on."

Becky likes working outside, taking in the fresh air, getting her hands dirty, and seeing small plants grow into big, flowering ones. Once the work is done, Becky and Steve enjoy surveying their progress and watching the birds, bees, insects, and other creatures at home in the yard.

For her designing and quilting, Becky's greatest inspiration comes from the plant colors in her garden. Her partner in Piece O' Cake Designs, Linda Jenkins, does a lot of floral appliqué. She agrees with Becky when she says, "It's amazing what you see when you pay attention!" Both artists find that the structure of plants and flowers contribute to their pattern designs, too.

Tip In the backyard, a small basket mounted on a fence post contains fabric scraps. Becky likes to use the scraps to tie her plants to supporting stakes. The birds use the scraps for their nests.

Still Life #1

BECKY GOLDSMITH
21 1/2" x 28 1/2"

Still Life #1 showcases both Becky's garden and her appliqué talents. The colors in the bouquet are reminiscent of autumn in her yard—vivid. She worked with hand-dyed solid cottons except for two prints used for the center of the yellow flower. Machine-quilting in the solid fabrics adds texture and dimension to the still life.

STILL LIFE #1

Materials

- $^2/_3$ yard for background
- 9" x 10" rectangle for vase
- Scraps of fabric for flowers and foliage (refer to the photograph)
- $^1/_8$ yard gold for border
- $^1/_8$ yard green for border
- Scraps of golds, greens, and turquoise for pieced border
- Two fat quarters (18" x 22") for piped binding. (You can get by with less if you don't mind lots of seams. Fat quarters utilize the fabric best with fewer seams.)
- 3 yards of cording (to insert in the binding)
- 1 yard for backing
- 26" x 33" batting

Appliqué Supplies

Becky and her partner, Linda Jenkins of Piece O' Cake Designs, Inc., have written *The Appliqué Handbook*, which is a great reference for appliqué. They find the supplies listed below useful.

- 100% cotton thread, 50 weight, in colors to match appliqués (Becky likes DMC machine embroidery thread)
- John James Size 11 straw needles or Size 12 sharps (the finer the needle, the less visible the stitch)
- $^1/_2$"-long sequin pins
- Bias bars for making stems and vines
- White chalk pencil
- Quilter's mechanical pencil

- Permanent fine-point marker
- Thimble (optional)
- Thimble-It finger protector pads (optional)
- Sharp-pointed scissors
- Circle template
- Clear upholstery vinyl (size of appliqué)
- Clear self-adhesive laminating sheets for templates
- Sandpaper board (to hold background fabric stable)

Cutting

Enlarge appliqué pattern 200%.

Cut background 21$^1/_2$" x 26$^1/_2$". (It will be trimmed to 20$^1/_2$" x 25$^1/_2$" after the appliqué is done.)

For bottom border, cut one 1$^1/_2$" x 20$^1/_2$" strip of green.

For left side and top borders, cut one 1" x 26$^1/_2$" strip and one 1" x 21" strip of gold.

For the piped edge, cut 1"-wide bias strips and piece to make 54$^1/_2$"-long strips from each print.

Cut 108" of cording.

Cutting sizes for pieced borders are given in the instructions.

Instructions

1. Prepare an overlay of the enlarged drawing on the clear vinyl using the permanent black pen. (The vinyl comes with a tissue-paper liner sheet.) Keeping the vinyl and tissue together, cut a 17" x 22" piece. Transfer dotted horizontal and vertical positioning lines from the pattern onto the vinyl at the top and bottom and at each side using a permanent marker.

2. Mark the appliqué design on the vinyl using a permanent marker.

3. Fold background fabric in half lengthwise and crosswise, and then lightly press on the fold lines. These folds will line up with the positioning lines on the pattern.

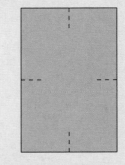

4. Matching the positioning lines, place the background fabric under the vinyl but atop the tissue-paper liner.

5. To make the templates, make five copies of the pattern (page 121) each at 200 percent. (You need five copies so you can cut each flower part and leaf as one piece.) Make sure the copy machine is accurate, neither stretching nor reducing the design. Peel off the backing on the self-adhesive laminating sheet, and lay the sticky side up, facing you.

Smooth each pattern, face down atop the sheet; pattern lines will face the sticky surface. Turn over the laminating sheet so you can see the lines, and cut out the templates. Place the templates right side up on the right side of the appropriate fabric and trace around with the chalk pencil. Cut out $^3/_{16}$" beyond the chalk line; the $^3/_{16}$" margin is the seam allowance.

6. Finger-press the chalk line under the edge of appliqué piece #1. Keep curves smooth and points sharp. Lift up the vinyl and place the piece on the background fabric, lining it up with the vinyl drawing. Pin in place.

7. Thread a needle with 18" of thread in a color that matches the appliqué. (Avoid lengths greater than 18"; they will fray and tangle.)

8. Use the needleturn appliqué technique, relying on the needle to turn under the seam allowance of the appliqué as you move along. (The thread will not show on the top of the fabric.) Begin on a straight edge rather than in a corner.

To stitch, bring the needle up at the edge of the appliqué (where you have turned under the seam allowance), through the background fabric and the appliqué. Take the needle straight down close to your stitch so that very little thread remains on the top of the fabric. Rock the needle forward, taking a small stitch, and come back up through the appliqué. The thread travels on the under side of the background. Keeping stitches uniform, take one stitch at

a time. Use your needle to turn under the appliqué seam allowance as you go along. Once you get into a rhythm you can relax and enjoy the process.

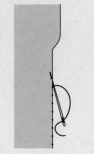

9. When you near an inner curve, stop before you get there and clip to the drawn line of the inner point. To prevent fraying, do not overwork this seam. The seam allowance will narrow as you approach the clipped point. Keep taking stitches, making sure you take one at the innermost point. This stitch will come a bit farther into the appliqué but will secure the clipped fabric.

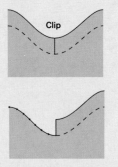

Take a stitch at the innermost point.

Continue to turn under seam allowance and stitch.

10. For an outer point, stitch to the point and stop where the two lines meet. Make a tack stitch over the last stitch just made.

Using your needle, tuck under the seam allowance at the point. Turn the appliqué in your hands and, again using the needle, turn under the seam allowance on the other side of the point and start stitching.

Note where two stitching lines will meet.

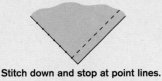

Stitch down and stop at point lines.

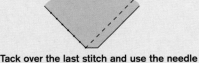

Tack over the last stitch and use the needle to tuck under the point of the seam allowance.

Turn under seam allowance on the other side and continue stitching.

11. To end the thread, bring the needle to the wrong side. Take an anchor stitch inside the appliqué on the background fabric.

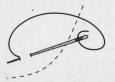

Bring needle to wrong side.

Make a tack stitch.

12. Continue appliquéing pieces in numerical order.

13. When the appliqué is finished, place it right side down on a towel to prevent flattening, and press.

14. Trim the background block to 20 $1/2$" x 25 $1/2$".

15. Stitch 1$1/2$" x 20 $1/2$" green strip to the bottom of the quilt and press.

16. Stitch 1" x 26 $1/2$" gold strip to the left side of the quilt and press.

17. Stitch 1" x 21" gold strip to the top of the quilt and press.

18. The pieced right border measures 1 $1/2$" x 27". Follow the cutting measurements and piecing guide below. Sew pieces together as shown and stitch to the right side of the quilt. Press.

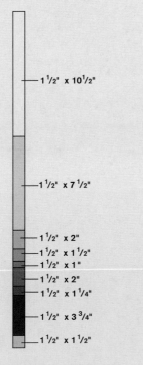

— 1$1/2$" x 10$1/2$"

— 1$1/2$" x 7 $1/2$"

— 1$1/2$" x 2"
— 1$1/2$" x 1 $1/2$"
— 1$1/2$" x 1"
— 1$1/2$" x 2"
— 1$1/2$" x 1 $1/4$"

— 1$1/2$" x 3 $3/4$"

— 1$1/2$" x 1 $1/2$"

Cutting measurements for right border

19. The second bottom border measures 2 $1/2$" x 22". Follow the cutting measurements and piecing guide.

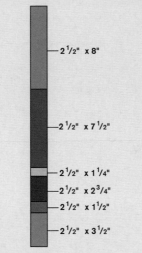

— 2 $1/2$" x 8"

— 2 $1/2$" x 7 $1/2$"

— 2 $1/2$" x 1 $1/4$"
— 2 $1/2$" x 2 $3/4$"
— 2 $1/2$" x 1 $1/2$"
— 2 $1/2$" x 3 $1/2$"

Cutting measurements for bottom border

Sew the pieces together as shown, stitch to the bottom of the quilt, and press.

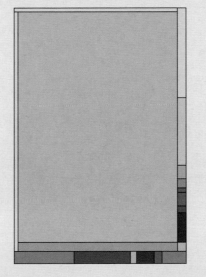

20. Layer the quilt and machine- or hand-quilt the interior appliqué area but not the borders. The designs Becky used for the background, vase, and yellow petals are on page 120. Refer to the photograph for the detail lines on the leaves. Once it is quilted, trim off the excess batting.

21. To make the piped edge, join the two lengths of bias strips together. Wrap the fabric over the cording as shown.

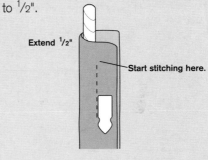

22. Starting $1/2$" from the end of the cording, machine-stitch fabric over cording using a zipper foot. Trim seam allowance to $1/2$".

Extend $1/2$"

Start stitching here.

23. To add piping to the quilt top, pin backing fabric away from the raw edges. Stitch piping to the quilt front, raw edges even. Allowing 4" of piping to remain free above start of seam, begin stitching on the left side of the quilt, where the second border meets the first. Round the corners by gently clipping three or four times into the seam allowance of the piping.

Clip

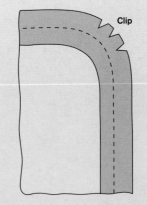

24. As you near the starting point, stop about $1/2$" away. Remove fabric from around the cording (pick out a few stitches) and trim the ends of the cord so they butt together. Encase ends of cording in fabric by turning under the raw edge of the uppermost fabric layer to hide raw edge of the lower layer. Finish stitching cording to quilt top.

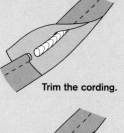

Trim the cording.

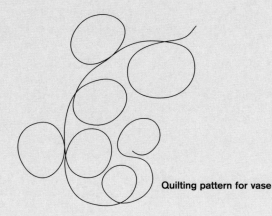

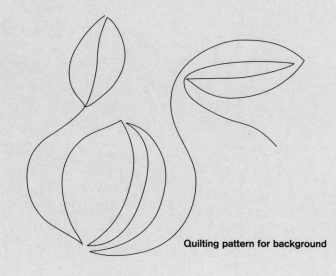

Quilting pattern for background

Fabric folds under and cording butts together.

25. Remove the pins from the backing fabric. Turn under the seam allowance and hand-stitch to the cording. This folded edge will rest on top of the piping stitching line.

26. Finish quilting the borders using the quilting patterns shown (right). Bind the quilt.

Quilting pattern for vase

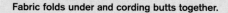

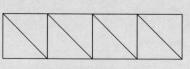

Quilting pattern for border

Quilting pattern for large flower

Quilting pattern for center of large yellow flower

Enlarge 200%

JEAN WELLS

Sisters, Oregon, USA

A Garden Through the Seasons

I n this rural paradise, Jean Wells has enhanced the natural beauty of the ponderosa pines, junipers, and wildflowers, using a quilter's touch to turn her acreage into a succession of unique gardens. Against the backdrop of the Three Sisters Mountains, this country setting boasts wildflowers of all kinds and old-fashioned flowers like hollyhocks, echinacea, gloriosa daisies, bleeding hearts, and peonies. Until mid-June this mountain setting can still have temperatures into the low thirties so perennials have to be hardy. Frost comes again in late August or early September, so the warm season is short.

The high-desert climate is perfect for Jean's two passions, gardening and quilting. Summers see her in the garden early in the morning, then off to her businesses, The Stitchin' Post quilt shop and The Wild Hare, a garden gift and accessory store. In the warm evenings, she is back in the garden, dreaming of her next project. She conceptualizes quilts, develops color combinations, and auditions design elements. By fall, she is ready to move to the studio that overlooks the garden and begin work on the plans developed in the summer.

When seed catalogs arrive after Christmas, while the snow is still on the ground, Jean begins dreaming again of her garden and ideas for the following summer. Perhaps there are new varieties of zinnias and sunflowers to try. Perhaps it is time to fine-tune a flowerbed. The warm sunny days of summer seem far away. Quilting fills the time not spent in the garden. Both endeavors feed the soul of this creative woman.

Once the daffodils bloom, wild field daisies and purple wallflowers blanket the garden. A sea of purple and white surrounds the approach to the house. Birds make their nests and the babies test their wings. Spring has arrived.

The pond took three years to build. The first year, wildflower seeds were sprinkled around the perimeter. The second year, the lupine took over the banks. The variety of colors in the lupine is astounding, inspiring daughter Valori's quilt. During the summer months Jean tucked mint plants into the rocks and added wild grass that she dug from a nearby river. Her dad gave her yellow iris and gold fish from his pond. As the years have gone by and the plants have filled in, the pond has developed a natural look. It has become a peaceful setting only two miles from Sisters.

Warm summer weather brings on more flowers. Red poppies and blue bachelor's buttons replace the spring purples. Butterflies appear almost like magic to add their color and shape to the garden.

In quilting, "transition colors" are those that take us from one color family to another. Green is constant in the garden, and the bright flower colors act as transitions, changing daily in the summer months.

By mid-July the garden has turned to yellow and white with touches of pink. Shasta daisies, the first flowers she planted, stand five feet high. Yarrow, Shasta daisies, and pink coneflowers (echinacea) give the picket fence area a new look. Paths lead from garden to garden. One late-summer day a baby garter snake climbs a gloriosa daisy stalk to sun himself. This small creature eats bugs, too. What a sight to see!

Red geraniums brighten a shady spot on a bench near the front porch. Jean winters over her geraniums, cutting them back in the fall and relocating them inside. There they start to leaf out and produce blooms, bringing part of the garden indoors during the long winters. They are a constant reminder of summer.

Several years ago Jean started experimenting with small "music box" sunflowers in planter boxes. Knowing how the deer, who are frequent visitors, like the new buds, she was unsure how to bring the buds to bloom. The answer was to plant so many that the deer were distracted. They grow in the fenced-in vegetable garden, along the house, and in their own separate garden, a thirty foot space where over twenty-five varieties of sunflowers thrive. A pathway leads to a bench in the center, a spot to sit in the "sunflower forest." When the flowers are developing buds for future blooms, they are draped in bird netting, which keeps the deer from eating the buds for dessert. In the fall, birds and gray squirrels feast on the seeds. Uneaten seeds grow the next spring, often in surprising places.

"Simplicity" best describes the winter garden—a single birdhouse on a tree, an empty bench in the sunflower garden, dried hops on the trellis, and a deserted herb garden. Snow blankets the ground, creating a serene landscape. Warm brown foliage appears through the neutral gray and white of the winter environment. Seeing the garden at rest allows Jean to dream about what she will do when spring comes and her creativity spreads outdoors.

Lettuce in the Garden

JEAN WELLS
38 1/2" x 38 1/2"

Lettuce In The Garden (Let Us) is a play on words. In my fenced-in vegetable garden there are always wild cottontail rabbits lurking through the fence. I dressed the rabbits trying to get into the vegetable garden in camouflage (lettuce leaves), chasing around the border. The pieced first border represents the fence with a rust stripe and lettuce fabric. Light brown and beige squares pieced on the diagonal form the garden background. Carrots, beets, and lettuce grow in peace surrounded, in my real-life garden, by sunflowers, sugar peas, and sweet-pea vines. My garden is an eclectic combination of all the things I don't want to feed to the rabbits or deer.

☙ LETTUCE IN THE GARDEN

☙ Materials

- $1/4$ yard each of two light beiges for the background
- $1/8$ yard each of five beiges and light browns for background
- $1/2$ yard rust for the first and third borders
- $3/4$ yard lilac for the second border
- $1/4$ yard each of four greens to represent lettuce colors, for the rabbits, first border, vegetable foliage, and lettuce
- $1/4$ yard of a rusty-style green for the lettuce and rabbit
- $1/8$ yard for carrots
- $1/8$ yard for beets
- $3/8$ yard for binding
- $1 1/4$ yards for backing
- 42" x 42" batting
- 2 yards lightweight paper-backed fusible web
- Six-strand embroidery floss in colors to match appliqués, for hand-buttonhole stitching. For machine-buttonhole stitching, the YLI Jeans Stitch thread works well.
- Quilting thread in a contrasting color, for lettering in the third border.

☙ Cutting

Cut the beiges and light browns into $2 3/4$" strips, then cut these into squares. You will have a few extra but this leaves room for decision-making.

For the first border, cut two $1 1/2$"-wide rust strips and two $1 1/2$"-wide green strips.

For the second border, cut four 6"-wide strips into two $23 1/2$" pieces for side borders and two $34 1/2$" pieces for top and bottom borders.

For the third border, cut four $2 1/2$"-wide rust strips into two $34 1/2$" side borders and two $38 1/2$" top and bottom borders.

Appliqué Shapes

Appliqué patterns are on pages 133-135. Trace the following on the paper-side of the paper-backed adhesive: three lettuce, one of which is reversed; seven carrots; three beets; six rabbits for the left side; and six rabbits for the right side. The dotted lines on the patterns indicate where pieces overlap.

☙ Instructions

1. On a flannel board or flat surface, arrange the beige and brown squares eight across and eight up-and-down on-point.

2. Stitch the blocks in each row together in a diagonal set, and press. Join rows together, and press.

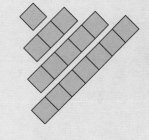

3. Using a ruler, mark a line 21" long on each edge. Stay-stitch (a single line of stitching) on this line to stabilize the bias of the squares. Using a ruler, measure $1/4$" outside this line, and trim off the excess fabric. This square will measure $21 1/2$".

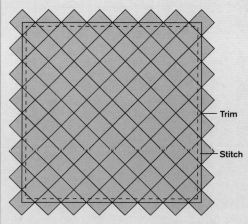

Trim

Stitch

4. Trim around the appliqué shapes, leaving a bit of paper beyond the pencil line. Place the adhesive side of the appliqué atop the wrong side of the appropriate fabric and press, following manufacturer's instructions. Cut around the appliqué shape on the pencil line. Peel off the paper. Referring to the photograph of the quilt, place the appliqués on the quilt and fuse in place following the manufacturer's instructions.

5. Either machine- or hand-buttonhole stitch around the appliqués. Jean hand-stitched the appliqués on this quilt.

To buttonhole stitch, use two strands of floss. Knot the end of the thread. Working from the fabric back, bring the needle up at the edge of the appliqué. Insert the needle down through the appliqué about 1/8" from the folded edge. (This distance will vary with the size of the appliqué.) Bring it back up through the background fabric at the edge of the appliqué, carrying the tip of the needle over the working thread. Pull the stitch into place until the thread is firmly in place and secure.

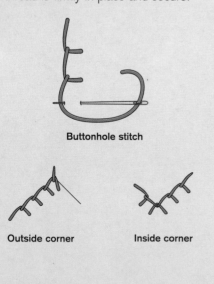

Buttonhole stitch

Outside corner   **Inside corner**

Holding the working thread with your left thumb, re-insert the needle into the applique about 1/8" from the first stitch and complete the next buttonhole stitch. Continue stitching, keeping the stitches proportional to the size of the motif. Vary the width and length of the stitches from motif to motif as appropriate. Note the illustrations showing where to place stitches for inside and outside corners.

6. Stitch the first border strips together, alternating the colors (rust, green, rust, green). Press seams in one direction. Cut across the strips at 1 1/2" intervals. Piece together strips of four squares, to make two side borders of 21 squares each and the top and bottom borders of 23 squares each. (If necessary, remove squares to ensure the side borders begin and end

with green squares and top and bottom borders begin and end with rust squares.)

Stitch strip sets to sides, then to the top and bottom of the quilt.

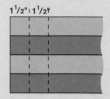

1 1/2" 1 1/2"

7. Stitch the second border to the sides, then to the top and bottom.

8. Arrange the rabbit appliqués around the second border and fuse into place. Buttonhole stitch around them.

9. Stitch the third border to the sides, then to the top and bottom.

10. Before the top is layered, trace the lettering "lettuce in the garden" around the edge of the third border using a chalk pencil.

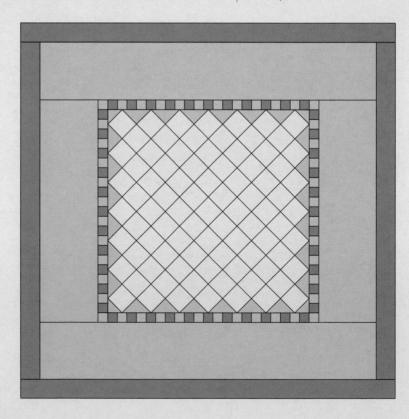

11. For quilting, outline all of the appliqué shapes and stitch-in-the-ditch along the seam lines in the borders. (Then you can echo-quilt around the appliqués, filling in the background. Jean, however, did not echo-quilt here. She used diagonal quilting along the seams of the background squares.) Finally, using a contrasting thread, stitch the lettering on the quilt.

Carrot
Cut 7

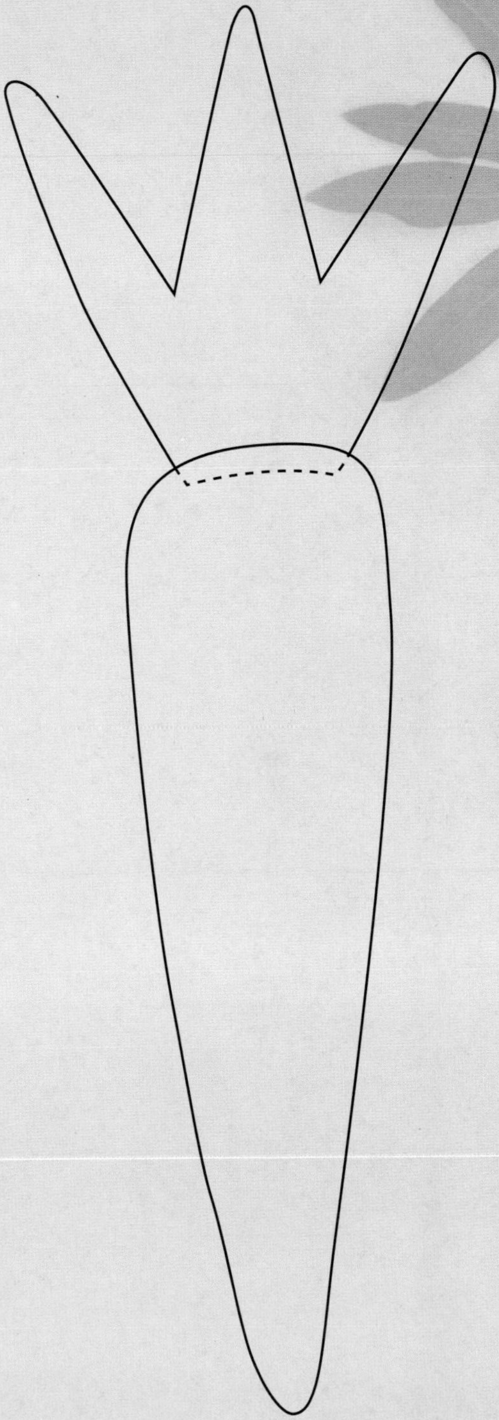

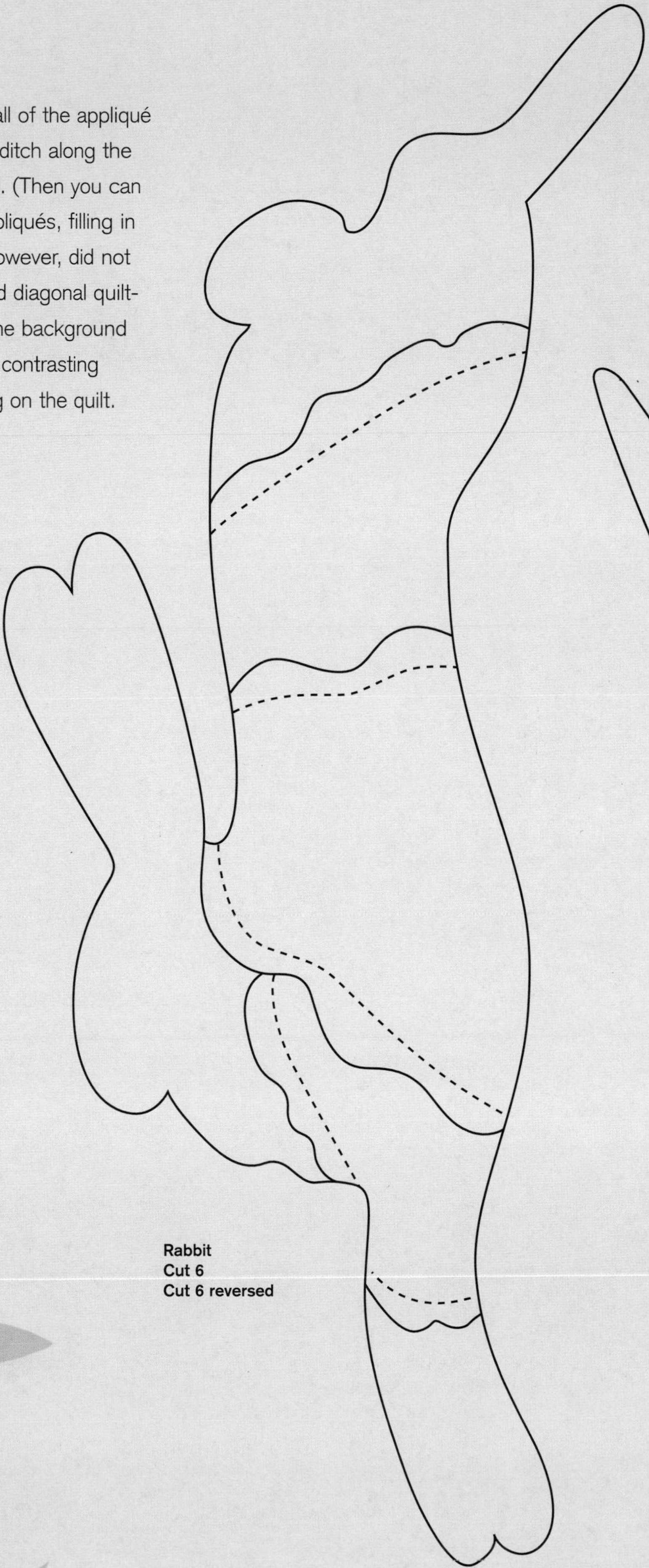

Rabbit
Cut 6
Cut 6 reversed

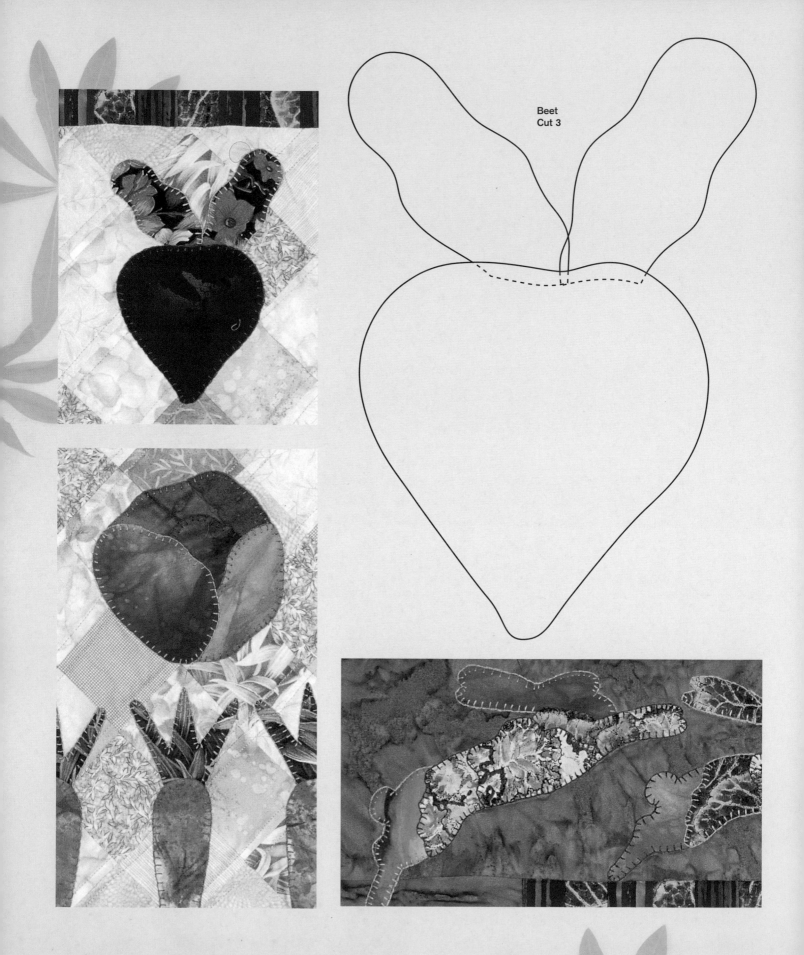

Beet
Cut 3

Lettuce
Cut 2
Cut 1 reversed

Tango in the Garden

VALORI WELLS
92 1/2" x 92 1/2"

The lupine growing in Jean's yard, which Valori has been photographing every spring for years, inspired this quilt. Valori loves the shape of the flowers and the way the colors graduate through the blossoms. These beauties captivated her imagination; she wanted to capture their essence in a pieced quilt design. Her photographs gave Valori all the color information she needed—the flowers were primarily purple, fuchsia, melon, and yellow. The challenge was to find a quilting technique.

Valori selected a Jacob's Ladder block as the foundation for the piecing, rearranging two units into half-square triangles and Four-Patches to represent the way she saw the flowers growing. The blocks are on-point and the center medallion consists of half-square triangles without the Four-Patches. The quilting was the icing on the cake for Valori. It was her way to express the lupine shapes in the quilt. Once the quilt was done she found that she didn't have a name. Jean's comment that it looked like music in the garden inspired *Tango in the Garden* because for Valori the quilt resembles the dramatic dance.

☙ TANGO IN THE GARDEN

☙ Materials

Valori used the lupine photographs to choose her colors. Selecting several different fabrics for each color group makes the quilt interesting.

- 4 yards total of green for piecing, border, and binding
- 1 $\frac{1}{3}$ yards total purple
- 1 yard total fuchsia
- $\frac{7}{8}$ yard total salmon/melon
- $\frac{3}{4}$ yard total yellow
- $\frac{7}{8}$ yard total of red violet
- 8 yards for backing
- 96 $\frac{1}{2}$" x 96 $\frac{1}{2}$" batting
- Optional: 4" finished half-square-triangle paper (170 units)

☙ Cutting

Referring to the quilt, sort fabrics for the half-square triangle units and Four-Patch units.

Cut twenty-two 4 $\frac{7}{8}$"-wide strips into 170 squares, each 4 $\frac{7}{8}$" square. Cut in half diagonally.

Or, follow the instructions on the half-square triangle paper. You will make 170 half-square triangle units.

Cut thirty-six 2 $\frac{1}{2}$"-wide strips into 2 $\frac{1}{2}$" squares. You will need 568 squares for 142 Four-Patch blocks.

Cut eleven 7 $\frac{1}{4}$" squares, then cut each into quarter-square triangles, to make 44 setting triangles.

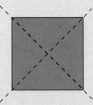

Cut two 7 $\frac{1}{2}$" squares, then cut each in half diagonally for corners.

For the border, cut thirty green 10" squares. Cut each in half diagonally. Cut three green and three deep purple squares, each 10 $\frac{3}{8}$"; cut these squares into quarter-square triangles.

☙ Instructions

1. Create half-square triangles in one of two ways: use triangle paper, following

the manufacturer's instructions, or follow the directions below. For either method, refer to the photograph for pairing ideas. To make the half-square triangles the traditional way, pair up two triangles, right sides together. Stitch together on the diagonal seam, and press seam to darker color. Make 170 triangle-squares.

2. For the Four-Patch blocks, pair up the squares and stitch them together. Continue sewing two pairs together to make 142 Four-Patches.

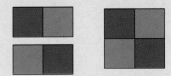

3. Following the quilt illustration and referring to the color photograph, place the blocks on a design wall. When you are satisfied with the arrangement, insert the setting triangles. (You will add the corners later.)

4. Stitch the quilt together in diagonal rows. Add the corner triangles, which will be a little too large. Press, then square up the corners. Trim the sides as shown.

¹/₄"

Trim to ¹/₄" beyond point.

5. For the border, complete 24 half-square triangle units. The other 12 triangles will be used for the squares with the accent color. Stitch the two smaller triangles together, then join them to the larger triangle.

6. Arrange the border squares around the quilt. Stitch eight top and bottom units together and add to the quilt. Stitch ten side units together and add to the quilt.

7. Valori's free-motion quilting designs for lupine leaves and flower stalks are on pages 139-140.

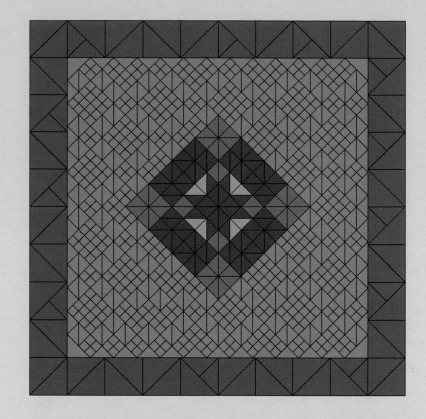

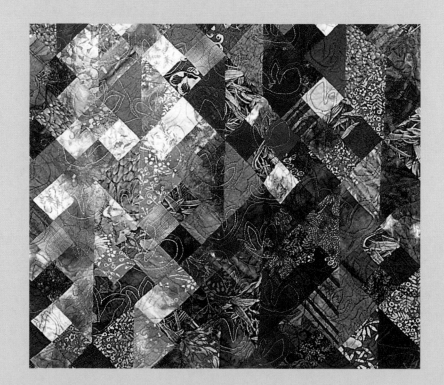

Quilting pattern for quilt center

Quilting pattern for quilt border

About the Authors

Jean and Valori, a well-known mother/daughter team, have come together to write their third book, *Along the Garden Path*. Working in the gardening and quilting fields agrees with this team. Valori focuses her talents through the lens of the camera, capturing gardens in unexpected ways. Her close-up, intimate, and landscape photographs bring inspiration to many a quilter. These experiences influence her in quilting, and you can see her interpretations of garden colors and shapes in fabric. Shapes seen in plants become quilting designs to expand the theme.

Valori's garden photography has also found a home in the textile industry with Quilters O.N.L.Y. Her photographs have inspired five collections of fabric, greeting cards, gift wrap, and a calendar. She joined her mother's business, The Stitchin' Post in Sisters, Oregon, two years after graduating from Pacific Northwest College of Art, where she received the "Outstanding Photographer" award.

Jean's love of sewing and teaching led her into the quilting world twenty-six years ago when she opened her quilt shop, The Stitchin' Post. Instructing others has been the main focus of everything she does, whether it be writing twenty-one how-to quilt books, designing fabric, appearing on "Simply Quilts," writing numerous articles for magazines, or teaching business and quilting workshops throughout the U.S. and Europe. In 2000, her business in Sisters, Oregon received the "Business of the Year" award. She has also received the Michael Kile Award for Lifetime Achievement in the quilting industry and been inducted into the Primedia Hall of Fame as one of the first "Independent Retailers."

Gardening became her outlet from all of the quilt-related activities that she does—now the two overlap. Her second retail store, The Wild Hare, is known for its unique garden-related decorative items, as well as the tools and supplies needed for creative gardening. In the summer Jean is in the garden dreaming up her next quilt. In the winter, Jean is thinking about how she will plant her vegetable garden or make changes in her two-acre plot. Jean's two interests keep her busy and creative.